What people are saying about Angie…

"Praises for *Full Circle*: it is Angie's gift of her unedited world. Like honey written with pure honesty, humility and the Angie Le Mar humour that we know and love. Page-turners are usually synonymous with salacious activity but this book will quench your thirst, soothe your soul and jump-start the dreams you are sitting on—Amen, Sister Angie!"

Beverley East, author of *Reaper of Souls* and *Finding Mr. Write*

"Angie's dad taught her, 'Whatever you start, finish'. I started Angie's book and I had to finish it! From the genesis to the end, I was gripped. Each word and chapter allowed me to get to know the 'Queen' who I have always admired and seen as my own mentor. Her journey in finding herself speaks to all hearts. This is not just an autobiography, but a memoir of how to love and accept self, and most importantly how to 'let go and let God'. A heartfelt reflection of her life, Angie's story is also a black British history lesson of those who paved the way not only for the current new kids on the comedy block, but also in theatre, radio and TV. *Full Circle* is a beautiful tribute to all those who have helped and inspired Angie, illustrating that 'behind every strong black woman, is a strong black man'. This is a must-read for the entire community teaching 'never, never give up!'"

Janelle Oswald, multi award-winning freelance journalist, columnist, presenter, broadcaster and photographer

"Captivating, nostalgic and, of course, funny. A rare opportunity to read the journey and delve into the mind and soul of one of the UK's creative geniuses."

Jackie G Michaels, editor-in-chief, *My Executive Lifestyle* Magazine

"Angie Le Mar is seriously funny. What an oxymoron! Yes, she is serious. Her stories are captivating, real and hold so many powerful life principles, and at the same time they are funny, which makes those truths easy to digest by all, young and old."

Pastor Nembhard, senior leader, the ARC

"Angie's book reads like a chocolate Bounty bar, to be savoured and enjoyed like a rare treat...and for those who remember the much beloved sweet crusted peanut rings that made the *crr crr* sound from back in the day, Angie's book will take you down memory lane, sharing the experience of a unique generation with her original humour, her honest tears of courage and definitely her tears of laughter..."

Treva Etienne, actor, writer, director

"*Full Circle* is a candid snapshot into the life of one of the UK's pioneering black comediennes. Readers meet Angie from the moment she takes her first breath, and travel with her throughout childhood as she discovers and nurtures her calling. Angie holds nothing back and is uninhibited in her narration of her rise to the top and quest to share her gift with the world. *Full Circle* is a story about persistence and sheer determination, one of laughter and one of sadness, one of lessons and one of success. But overall, it's one of faith."

Dionne Grant, journalist

"Angie is a positive and empowering influence. I have watched over the years as she supported and encouraged others. Her giving nature continues with every word in this book. It is a candid and insightful journey, tinged with humour; a story which I am sure will inspire many!"

Grace Ononiwu, OBE

About Angie

Angie Le Mar—the multi-award winning comedienne, businesswoman, speaker, writer, director, producer and talk show host—blends her own style of creativity and fun with out of the box thinking to bring her own brand of entertainment straight to her audience.

As one of Britain's top comediennes, Angie has successfully harnessed the power of laughter to create inspiring and thought provoking productions. From stage to radio to TV to the written page, Angie is a proven hit with a multicultural audience—male, female, young and old alike. She is equally at home with quick-fire comedy, acutely observed character sketches, and solid acting performances.

Angie's wide ranging career achievements, from being the first British performer to storm the legendary Harlem Apollo, to making history in London's West End with the first ever sell out show by a black comedienne, not only enables her to deliver top-quality performance and production values on stage, screen and the airwaves, but also to attract a large and loyal fan base along with greatly increased audiences wherever her work appears.

Angie is married with three children.

Angie Le Mar is a well sought-after speaker. An entrepreneur and business woman, with a great knowledge of the creative indrustries, she has overcome enormous obstacles to achieve her highest goals. A inspiration to many people, a story filled with great optimism, laughter and, above all, hope. As a motivational speaker, she shares her story and expertise so that others may go on to achieve their greatest dreams.

More information, please contact www.angielemar.com

FULL CIRCLE

BY ANGIE LE MAR

Published by Filament Publishing Ltd

16 Croydon Road, Beddington, Croydon,

Surrey, CR0 4PA, United Kingdom.

+44(0)20 8688 2598

www.filamentpublishing.com

ISBN 978-1-911425-73-1

Book Cover Credit
Photography: Elin Robinson
Stylist: Sophia Powell
Hair: MzHair Ltd
Make-up: Emma McRae Fashion Fair

This book is dedicated to my wonderful loving father,
Raglan George Martin. I'm glad we both knew how important
we were to each other, and more importantly that our love for each other
was just so special.

I'm sorry you have gone, but glad that you were here.
Always in my heart. A x

CONTENTS

Foreword

As a journalist, script editor, producer and general cheerleader for the entertainment industry via my work at *The Stage* newspaper and elsewhere, I've had the privilege of working with Angie Le Mar for close to 20 years on many different projects. I would like to think that this is because of my good looks, talent and charm…but I suspect it is more due to the fact that I am one of the few people on earth who can read her handwriting.

It's always struck me as ironic that many of the best writers and creators I have worked with struggles with dyslexia—and Angie is right up there with the best as far as I am concerned—but it's equally fascinating how God can take challenges that you might think would shut down somebody's progress in life and turn them into a means of going beyond what the world thinks is possible.

It's certainly something I experienced very soon after meeting Angie. Having grown up with, worked with, written for radio and TV and otherwise lived with comedy for more than 50 years, there are not many comedy routines or jokes I can't predict the punchlines to (which makes me a pain to go to the movies with), but Angie has always been able to actually make me laugh. Not the polite professional laughter of, "That's a good joke, let's keep it in the script," but the uncontrollable belly laugh of, "Angie, only YOU could come up with that one!"

Scientists will tell you that people with dyslexia are good at this because they think in a wonderfully 'sideways' and creative way, but with Angie I think that's only half the story; she is not only one of the funniest people I know but also one of the most serious and caring people I know—her best comedy often comes from taking the deepest, most personal and sometimes the most uncomfortable truths and having the courage to put them out there where, through the healing power of laughter, they can no longer hold us back or divide us because we think we are the only one who has ever had that doubt, that fear, that insecurity.

I think that's why Angie is so much in demand to speak at churches. There are some who deride 'Christian comedy' as something not very good comedians do because they can't handle the toughness of the real comedy circuit and 'church audiences don't throw bottles'. As you'll hear in Angie's story, in this case that stereotype couldn't be further from the truth: Angie has held her own as one of the very first black female comics not only in the toughest venues of the white male dominated mainstream circuit, but also as a pioneer of comedy in the black community in the days before there even was a comedy circuit.

For me, the evidence of God at work isn't so much that she took on the comedy and broadcasting worlds and conquered them: as I have already said, she has a God-given talent for writing which, combined with her hugely professional and hard-working attitude, would make her hard to ignore in any business. The miracle for me is that she has come through the hard road both on and offstage without becoming cynical and without becoming selfish. If there has been one constant in the many different projects I have seen Angie work on over the years, it has been the number of people young and old, black and white, famous and unknown she has taken the time to encourage, develop, motivate and—perhaps the most unusual trait of all in a comedian—simply listen to along the way.

Whether you have already listened to Angie in a club, on the radio, on TV, in a church or whether you are meeting her for the first time in these pages, I can guarantee you are going to have a funny, serious, thought-provoking and inspirational time. I know I am too, because even though I was around for many of the events in Angie's story, I'm pretty sure that just as she does with jokes, truths and timeless Christian principles, she'll find a way of presenting them in fresh new ways I have never thought of before.

And I'll probably find myself laughing out loud, just as I used to do when I finally managed to decipher what she had written in one of those early comedy scripts—another part of her story that has very definitely come full circle.

John Byrne

Prologue

"I've learnt that people will forget what you said, people will forget what you did, but people will never forget how you made them feel."

~ *Maya Angelou*

Well, I've written a book, I'm an author now and that's a fact. I have been asked a few times to write one, but a book was far from my mind! However when inspirational speaker and independent film maker Getrude Matshe contacted me and asked, "I've been on your website, where is your book?" that was the beginning of my journey. Stop, start, stop, start…stop, start… Finish.

It took me a while to believe I had something to share, not just on theatre, radio and TV, but in print. I am feeling excited about this new adventure and a bit nervous. But one thing I know for sure, nothing ventured, nothing gained. I have nothing to lose.

As you read my story, you'll see how I went for things at any age, even if I doubted myself. I tried a lot of things, succeeded at most, even in my own little way, or at least I gave it a go. I stripped naked. Okay, that sounds a bit dramatic, but it's daunting every single time I walk on stage as a stand-up comic: you don't know if it's going to work until the moment you hear laughter. But I love it and I know why. I love the sound of laughter and I appreciate how that makes everyone feel, so when I make people feel that, I know I am using my gift.

Being dyslexic is a gift as well. I thought it would hinder me but instead it pushed me forward because I do it differently from everyone else, and that's okay.

It takes a while to realise what your calling is, to understand and make it work for you. Once I got paid for telling jokes, I knew I'd found my career path. All I needed to know was that I could make a living making people laugh. Yes you can, yes you will, yes you did!

I am never going to worry. I go for things in life and believe that what is for you will be for you, I can't view it any other way. I learned that when I didn't get an audition, or something didn't work out, or a relationship ended, I didn't die.

I learned to take risks, trust my instincts and believe in myself whether I was standing in the school playground chanting or stepping out on the stage.

After losing my father, I realised that all the money and medication will not intervene when it is time for you to leave this earth. So I have decided to really make the effort to value every moment, give myself a pat on the back and say, '*Well done, love!*'

As I play back my memory's video tape, I don't think I appreciated some of the amazing experiences I have had, the places I've travelled to and the people I've met. I've done the first 50 years and I'm pretty excited about my new ventures, even if it's just running in the park with my granddaughters Tahlia, who wants to make people laugh, and baby Rhae. We are waiting to see what her plans are. Don't think I haven't thought about a sitcom with a glamorous grandma who has to raise her granddaughters! Always creating.

I promised my dad I would finish this book. He read some of it and loved it. My dad would say whatever you start, finish.

Well, I finished it, Dad!

I hope you enjoy.

Angie Le Mar, January 2017

Chapter 1:
A left-handed girl...Praise the Lord!

My mother had always wanted a little girl; she had three boys already and felt that was quite enough. I can understand that; she loved her boys but I think she needed a little pink in her life. So my mother did what any good Christian woman would do—she prayed. She prayed hard for a little girl, but no, that was not enough; she prayed that this little girl would be an actress. Yes, to fulfil her own dreams of being an actress. But still that wasn't enough...could this baby be a little girl maybe, and an actress, but—one more prayer—could she also be left-handed?

In the busy labour ward in 1965, the lights were set, the audience, doctors and nurses waited, and after a little push, there she was, a little left-handed girl, waiting for her close-up. Please welcome Angela Leonie Martin to the theatre! My Mother screamed, "PRAISE THE LORD!"

My older brother Michael always liked my humour, he picked up that I was very quick-witted. Too quick-witted—sometimes it would get me into trouble! I knew I was borderline cheeky. He'd always say in a very serious tone, "You're funny, you know." I'd think, '*Well, laugh then*'. My other brother Rohan would laugh, but Larry, the youngest of my brothers, would ignore me. He'd say, "Ah, she's not funny. She's stupid. I hate her." Such love!

So I never got a laugh from Larry, but Michael would always say, "Ah, you're funny, you're good. You say some stuff that other people wouldn't even be thinking about." I had no idea what he was talking about, but it made me feel good.

I used to entertain my brothers at home by pretending to be my mum and dad, like I would pretend to be my mum, put on a West Indian accent, and mimic her talking to Dad. I'd switch into character. "Martin, Martin, dinner, you ready for your dinner, it's going to get cold, come on nah man."

"I don't want nothing to eat, I'm alright, not ready for my dinner yet," I would reply in Daddy's deep, kind, loving voice.

So I'd be doing all these voices and putting them into the conversation, and my brothers used to think, *'Is she mad?'*

As I was growing up, they could see that I was a performer. I was in my own world and quite happy to be in my room by myself. I had my dolls for company and would let them talk—who knew, I was casting a long time ago.

My dolls were always talking! A typical conversation would go like this: "Why do we have to sit here and stare at you? Can you at least move us around the house?"

"But you can't go around by yourself. If you get near the paraffin heater, you'll melt."

"Well buy us some new clothes then. How long do we have to wear these same stinking clothes, and our knickers need changing, and some of us need to dodo, lady!"

I don't know how I sounded to my family. Inside the room, I was saying, "No, no, no…let's go to the toilet."

"But I've been to the toilet already. I can't go again."

See how easily scriptwriting came to me? That's because I was trained by my dolls; we were always talking. At nights they would talk to me in my head. As I lay in bed sometimes my dolls would scare me, because their eyes were closed or their eyes were open, and I'd think to myself, *'Alright sleep now, why are you awake, you little duppies?'* It's almost like they came to life. When they were sleeping, I'd be wondering, *'What are they thinking about?'* I'd ask myself questions: did I hurt Tiny Tears when I sliced her mouth? Is she going to wake up and go, "You slashed my mouth"? I'd watch all those psycho dolly films like *Chucky*, and I'd think, *'Oh God, it's too much; I can't take it, but it's all in my mind.'*

My teddy bears would look at me and talk to me, and I'd think, *'You're bored, aren't you, sitting there? Should I turn you so you can see that wall again?'* Silly things like that. I think my brothers thought I was funny and humorous but they also wondered how I could sit by myself and talk to myself, not needing their company.

I really do like my own company, that's never changed. I don't need a crowd to feel comfortable, I like the sound of sound. I'm not a loner, I enjoy people, but sometimes I'll be in a crowd and feel so awkward...small talk takes work for me. If you're up for talking then I am up for it, but talking for talking's sake can be draining sometimes.

A friend phoned me once and said, "You don't seem to want to come out, I notice you slipped away at that event." I had been caught showing my face then disappearing, my usual act.

"No, I don't like going out all the time, there's too much talking." That's what I'm like. Once I know what we have to do, can we just go and get on with it please? Do we really need another meeting and all that talking? Let's go and do now.

And I don't like to be in conversations all the time because I find they interrupt me, they stop me from thinking. If a joke is coming to me, or a funny thought, I don't want to miss it. It's like interrupting a big sneeze. I tried to explain this to a friend and she didn't understand what I was talking about. I said, "You're interrupting my space, I'm thinking." I don't think people understand that thinking needs space and that you need to allocate time for that.

I used to think a lot when I was a little girl; I'd think and think. My parents would ask, "Are you alright, Angie?"

"Yes, I'm thinking."

"Yeah, but what are you thinking about?"

"I don't know until I've thought about it."

I don't like it when people say, "What are you thinking? Penny for your thoughts."

'It costs more than a penny, mate.'

Chapter 2:
Tiny Tears

"Mum, I've got to have Tiny Tears."

"No, Angie, you have enough dolls."

Dad used to give me presents regardless of whether or not it was Christmas or my birthday. "Here you go, here's the money," he would say as I pleaded with him for the next item on my inexhaustible wish list. Dad was always the one who would say, "Here's a bit of pocket money, Angie." Having pocket money was not a black thing when I was growing up. It was always suggested but for some reason that weekly payment always seemed to get missed, or when you brought it to your parents' attention, it was greeted with one word… "Move!"

Every Thursday, my dad would bring me home a Bounty chocolate bar because that was the day he got paid. So we could expect chocolates on a Thursday. All of us would get a chocolate bar from Dad. He would say, "Here's a Bounty for you, a Mars bar for you." But it was the crusted peanut rings that were our favourite. This was the sweet that he'd bring home for Mum. You could hear her enjoying it, it made a *crr, crr* crunching sound. Farewell, false teeth.

I don't think Dad ever said no to me. It's always been, "Daddy, can I have ten pence to go and buy this or that? Please, Daddy, please, Daddy."

The only thing that would stop my dad from giving something to me was if my mum intervened, "No, don't give it to her," and I'd think, "Oh, that was so badly timed, I didn't know she was behind me." Mum would be the one to stop all those nearly-got-it moments; we always felt Daddy would have said yes if Mummy wasn't there.

When Mum said no to Tiny Tears, I wasn't surprised or even upset. This was the usual route, Mum first then Daddy. I gave her a chance to buy it for me, but no, she blew it, again...so, of course, I went to my dad. I would get my act together, my voice was in place, eyes on cute, I remember having this script ready, with the right soft little girl voice, "Daddy, can I ask you something? Okay, I love you, Dad. Daddy, could you buy me a doll, Tiny Tears, it's not expensive. The reason why I need Tiny Tears is because it's a special dolly, and if I don't get Tiny Tears, maybe this will be my last request, I don't want anything, you won't have to buy me anything again, everybody's got Tiny Tears. All my friends have got Tiny Tears, and I *need* Tiny Tears."

I could see the green dress with that sweet white stripe, those white puff sleeves. Tiny Tears didn't have long hair or anything; she was in a box, lonely, waiting for me to get my dad to understand that she was special, that she was my baby. She even had a dummy and she had nappies and stuff like that. You could feed her and she'd wet her nappy. I just wanted that responsibility. The wee-wee would come out. I would give her orange drinks as well as milk so I could get the wee colour right. I was so excited by the thought of being able to change this child, my child, and they had it in the sweet shop, and it was the last one left. I would go into the sweet shop and stare at Tiny Tears and think, '*I want Tiny Tears, I want Tiny Tears...*'

So Dad bought Tiny Tears. It was so cool walking to the shop with my dad to get this doll. He walked in, pointed at the doll and bought it, as cool as that, no words, just, here you go. Can this man stop being my hero for a second? Never!

I was so excited. I didn't enjoy just giving her the milk and having to change her. No, I thought, *'Tiny Tears is hungry and needs some food.'* So I took some Weetabix cereal and mixed it up, and got a razor blade and sliced Tiny Tears' mouth. I have no idea where that came from, I wasn't a troubled child, I had shown no signs of violence and had never been wicked or evil. I didn't watch many horror movies. I don't know where the confidence came from, but it was a natural thought. I just went into the bathroom and worked out where my dad kept his razor blades, skipped back to my room, very normal. I remember grabbing the doll, and looking at her, like, *'This may hurt but you'll thank me later'* and slicing her mouth, I squeezed her cheeks, just like that and spooned the Weetabix into her mouth thinking, *'I'm giving you more, they've said we should only give you milk, but I think I should give you more.'*

So I kept feeding her cereal. I was so happy with myself! I was making a difference to a doll's life, dolls' lives matter. As the days went by, Tiny seemed just a little ungrateful about what I was doing for her. Nothing in her life changed. Maybe she only wanted milk and I was just causing a problem here? I'd notice she wasn't weeing as expected; nothing was coming out, which caused me great concern. I watched her carefully until one day it hit me. *'The stink is coming from her, Tiny stinks, Tiny is constipated.'*

Then this dolly started to stink even more because the cereal was sitting inside her and the milk was rotting, her digestive system wasn't real, and if you keep milk in a warm confined space, it will need attention. I tried to squeeze her belly into submission, but there was no joy. I wondered if I could slice her bum, but I'd done enough slicing. No. I had to confess my sins, try to explain why I took my dad's razor blades from the bathroom to slice my doll's mouth. It was hard to explain it. My mum was annoyed; my dad gave me that 'you are odd' look. Mum had to take off Tiny Tears' legs and open her up. We scraped out all the stale Weetabix and sticky milk and washed Tiny Tears inside out.

When she went back to join the other dolls, you could see she felt a little insecure: how was she going to explain that Angie, their mother, had sliced her mouth? I turned the lights off and went downstairs to reflect upon my actions.

My mum, Olive Martin, three months pregnant with me.

Me at six months, outside the home we lived in with the
Hall family on Tyrwhitt Road.

Me with my mum and Deacon Allen from Brockley Church COGIC.
We were going to our church convention.

The family in the front room. Back: Michael, Mother, Father.
Front: Larry, me and Rohan.

Me with my best friend Pamela Donaldson outside church.

Chapter 3:
Sepia brothers

I was born the year before the only time England won the World Cup, Larry was born the year before me, both of us courtesy of Lewisham Hospital.

Larry and I were like twins. It was a love and hate relationship similar to the one most siblings have who are born close to each other. Often we felt like two kids living together; it was fantastic as we both had our own rooms. You have to understand; it was a very rare thing for children from black families in England to have their own rooms. Even families owning their home rather than renting it with others was rare; my parents had rented like that for a few years when they first came over here. It was standard for families from the Caribbean to live together; the rejection made them depend on each other so if you had a home, you'd rent out the rooms. My dad lived with his sister when he first arrived. After sending for my mother, the two of them moved in with Mr and Mrs Hall. As children, we had great memories; you had an instant family, whoever was living there became your siblings. Karen Hall was my older sister, we grew up very close. But my mum wanted her own place so she hunted until she found her dream home—luckily for us it was just around the corner, so Karen and I would remain close.

Larry and I left the Halls for our new home with our own bedrooms. We were scared until my parents started renting rooms which meant we went back to sharing.

Larry wasn't mad although he nearly killed me a few times. Once he found my mum's tablets and told me that these green tablets were Smarties. Not being smart, a family friend and I ate them. We were rushed to the hospital, where we were washed out or pumped.

Actually maybe he was mad because another time Larry gave me what I thought was a glass of water. It wasn't: it was turps, white spirit for paint. Needless to say, we were back down to Lewisham Hospital. I still can't understand why the smell or the taste didn't stop me, I guess I trusted him.

I believe we were so close because I survived all his attempts to kill me… But soon all this would change when the family got bigger almost overnight. I think we were four and five years old when our parents called us into the kitchen.

"Angie, Larry, come here. We have something to tell you both."

Dad looked at Larry and then back at me. He slowly unfolded his hands and laid his palms on his lap. In his calm voice, as if he was telling us something very ordinary, Dad said, "We've got some people coming to live with us. Your brothers are coming to live with us."

I'll never forget that moment. I was shocked. "What do you mean we've got brothers? Explain." I had one brother, Larry, and he was quite enough to be getting on with. He was my brother, how do you get brothers if you've not seen them before? It didn't make sense to me. Can't I just get brothers who are younger than I am?

Soon my confusion turned to excitement, and I said, "Wow, we have brothers! We're going to see our brothers!"

Larry and I jumped into the backseat of Dad's Triumph 2000 SEG 493G and began the drive to the airport. The excitement of going to pick up our brothers was almost too much for me to take in. I was excited and at the same time didn't know what to expect. We parked the car and waited at

Heathrow arrivals. Each person who turned the final corner out of Customs was potentially one of my brothers.

Then they came through. "Oh God, what is that? Those are our brothers?" They were two little boys, one taller than the other, dressed in small brown suits. They both sported sharp haircuts and wore immaculate black polished shoes. They looked completely different from any of the children I had ever seen…at least in Lewisham, South London! The suits were brownish charcoal grey and it was as if I was seeing them through a nostalgic sepia-coloured lens that sent me back in time, like in the old photos I had come across of Mum and Dad in the 1950s. These boys didn't look like Larry. Larry was my brother; I knew this because, well, he looked like me. But these two didn't. They just looked different. They looked very old; they didn't dress like us. I wondered why they were dressing like old men and where they were going with that odd-looking suitcase, which I later found out was called a grip!

I looked at them and felt, *'Urgh!'* I wanted better brothers. I certainly didn't want them. Give me brothers about whom I could say with pride: "These are my brothers." I couldn't introduce these sepia boys and tell people that they were my brothers.

When we got home, the whole house had to be changed because now I had to move in with Larry and share his bed. The other two, Michael, the eldest at age nine, and Rohan, who was six, got the other room. That was conflict right there.

Over the next few days, Larry and I were told by Mum that our brothers had been born when she was in Jamaica, but she couldn't bring them over until now. When Dad had sent for her to come to England, it was the chance of a new life, but they didn't have the income to support everybody over here at the beginning. Michael and Rohan had been left with my grandmother in Jamaica until Mum had enough money and the family could be reunited. It sounds a lot more romantic than it was.

Thinking back, I am sure that Mum and Dad had already told Larry and me that we had brothers. It was just that we were too young to understand what this meant. If we couldn't see it, it wasn't in our reality. I wondered how Mum must have felt seeing her sons again after being apart from them for six years. I bet the tears rolled down her cheeks and Larry and I were just too oblivious, excited or disappointed to notice.

"That boy's on my bike. Get him off my bike, Mummy."

"He's your brother, Angie."

"No, he's not my brother! My brother doesn't look like that. I can't accept him."

It took Larry and me a long time to accept our new brothers. I would call them 'that boy'. I never called them by their names, instead it was 'that boy', 'that boy there', 'those over there', 'them'. It had nothing to do with my brothers. I just think it took me a long time to connect with who they were. I think there was a little bit of a 'we were born here and you were born there' feeling for a long time. They felt it more because they thought that we got special treatment. I didn't see it because Mum was very fair, and I think she felt guilty. But it was never her fault; she did the best she could and raised us all with the same love.

The Jamaican brothers stuck close to each other for a long while, then as the years went by, they were no longer separate from us; we were now united. The thick Jamaican accent faded and the old-fashioned clothes slowly disappeared. The bonds changed over the years, our ages making all the difference: Michael had become the working brother and would be gone all day; this pleased us immensely as we no longer had duties to do and our ruler had gone, at least for most of the day. When that boy was away, I would sneak into his room with the Pioneer hi-fi, his room that always had money sprinkled all over the floor. Okay, maybe I looked in the drawers and went through his pockets; lucky for me, he never missed a penny.

Earth, Wind and Fire, the Brothers Johnson—those albums had such an impact, Bob Marley, Third World...my brother had them all. I danced, I mimed, I jump off the bed, I was in concert from 3.45 pm until 6.30 pm. On many occasions I would get caught, the giveaway was the overheated hi-fi. He'd call me into his room and ask, "Were you in my room?"

I'd look at him with disgust, hurt even, why would I be here, yes, a bit of an attitude!

"No."

"You're lying."

"Why would I lie? I don't need anything in here. This is a boy's room. I'm a girl!"

He would lead me to the hi-fi, touch it (yes, it was warm), and look at me. I would look back at him wondering whether or not he was going to hit me. He would tell me off, make a lot of noise, about his things, his things, that he can buy because he's working, he's better than us, because he's working, and we are the poor peasants waiting for his crumbs. Yes, we waited!

After that, he started to lock the door. It was time to let go of listening to The Investigators and Jean Adebambo and get on with my life. On the rare occasion that he'd forget to lock the door I would get in there, dance, take his money, cool the hi-fi and leave. Once I got my own hi-fi, I was gone next-door.

There's more. More brothers. "We are gathered here again to tell you that you have another brother."

Okay, what's going on? I'm trying to accept these funny fast-talking brothers and now you tell me there's more, well where is this one coming from?

"Are we going back to the airport?"

"No, not this time, this time we are going to the coach station because this brother lives in England, he's coming from Birmingham." A-ha, I thought, so there's an accent attached to this brother too.

This brother's name is Wayne, he was younger than Michael but he's not my mum's child. *'Okay...let's work this out again...'* I'm a young child trying to understand why Wayne looks exactly like Rohan but is not my mum's child... *'I need to lie down.'*

They called him the outside child, my brother was an outside child and although that sounds cruel, he's inside here, and we love him. *No, don't explain Mummy and Daddy, we get it and we accept it.* Wayne just slotted in, he now had siblings, so I guess we were like a breath of fresh air to him. I was truly spoilt by Wayne, he really loved me. I was a special sister to him, I was so grateful that I had another brother and bonding with him was easy.

"So is that it now, parents? No more surprises?"

"You have a sister in Jamaica too."

Stop it.

Chapter 4:
Summer holidays

Having Michael and Rohan living with us meant that Larry and I shared not only a double bed but also a purple quilt! Our room was large and spacious. It had a very big ottoman wardrobe at the bottom of a large antique bed; in fact, everything about our room was big and strong.

There was nothing childish about it; there were no ABC posters or the type of decorations that children have in their rooms today. Instead, it was functional with a feeling that everything in there was supposed to be in there.

One thing that was certain about our room, even with the two of us sharing it, was that it was sometimes bitterly cold in the winter months. We used a paraffin heater and would warm our hands over the metal bars until we could move our fingers again. It was always cold until it got very hot. There was no medium or slightly warm!

When it was very cold, we would get sent up to heat the rooms at a certain time, either Michael or Rohan and I would be told to go and put the heaters on because "in half an hour, you're all going to bed." So every winter there was always a time slot for that and Larry and I always used to fight about whose turn it was.

Sometimes it felt like we were in each other's skin. We were so close when we were young that I started to hate him for just growing up. We poked fun at each other, or, more accurately, Larry poked fun at me. He would call me names like 'Fatty this,' or 'Stupid Angie that.' Sometimes when we fought, I used to run after him with knives and everything! I wanted to kill him.

Summer holidays were the worst because it wasn't about going to adventure playgrounds or going out anywhere special; it was about staying at home all day until we found things to do. We had a list of things to do before the day started—clean the house, get our chores done—before any fun could be had. We were forbidden from going out into the front street until our parents came home from work, so everything happened in the house and garden. Friends weren't allowed in unless they were absolutely family.

The days were long in the summer but we weren't going on any holidays; we were just going to stay here and make our own fun.

First things first, we'd watch all the summer TV shows, *Why don't you...*, *The Double Deckers*, *Take Hart*, and once all those programmes were over, we were bored. A few more Elvis or Cliff Richards films, and we were done.

So into the garden we'd go, playing football and kicking up the newly laid lawn. I'd look for insects and leaves to make a home for them in my special jar where I'd pierced holes in the top so they could breathe.

Mum would leave the food out for us so our only thing to do was to play. I spent hours in the garden making little mud sandwiches for the ladybirds; this took up a lot of my time, getting the right consistency of mud and finding the right thickness of leaves to act as bread. I would find insects and feed them my mud sandwich. Everything was very simple and I was captivated. Today my mud sandwiches would be the equivalent of my son's PlayStation but *a lot* less expensive. Things change.

When I think about my relationship with Larry, I think we went from liking each other to not liking each other, back to liking each other. It's almost like we've gone back to how we were at the beginning. Because Larry was quite close to me, he got a bigger reaction from me, whereas Rohan used to be the one who always broke up the fights.

We were bored. If we went outside, what could happen? We'd only go to the park and get back before our parents and act like we'd just been playing at home. We would go and rush back, and not get caught. Those days, parents on the street were looking out for you—we had the Dixons, the Pascals, the Smalls and the Adams all looking out for each other. I don't think they knew it was called Neighbourhood Watch, they would just watch out for their neighbours, and that meant avoiding them. I'm sure my parents told the other parents these children are not meant to be outside so if you see them, let us know, and they did, but we never knew who it was, we just knew they were all in it together.

One evening Larry came running home screaming from the park. Rohan had been attacked; his head had been split open by a cricket bat. We were so scared when he was rushed to the hospital.

When Michael got home from work and found out about Rohan, he quietly changed his clothes and left the house. He went looking for our brother's assailant. I thought war was going to break out. He was so angry; I had never seen my brothers so emotional about each other. Larry had tried to fight the boy when it happened and now Michael was going to kill someone. I felt angry that would happen to my brother, so maybe I should get out there and fight, fight for the family; you don't mess with us!

Michael returned after a while. I wanted to shout, "Did you kill him? Are we the warriors going out to play? Do we have a war on our hands?"

No, we are not going out to play. My mum has completely banned outside activities unless we are going to church.

Chapter 5:
Michael

Michael thought he was a king; that was what I thought anyway. When Mum and Dad had left for work, he would cook a big fry-up and eat it slowly in front of Rohan, Larry and me. We would sit there pleading, "Oh, Michael, don't eat all the bacon, oh, don't eat all the sausage, oh, don't eat the plantain!"

You'd think there was no breakfast or food in the house, but we used to have cereal, tea, toast and maybe an egg. Since Michael was the oldest, he would fry up food only for himself; he was never going to make any for us. I would just sit there thinking, *'Thank God my mum doesn't know all this is happening.'* It would have traumatised her to know we were not getting any fry-up. It was only years later that we told her what had happened.

In the absence of our parents, Michael would be the one in charge, he gave us the rules. If anyone ever needs a slave master, he would qualify because he used to command us… "Angie, bathroom, toilet… Larry, dining room… Rohan, stairs, and when you've finished, call me!"

Brookbank Road was the street we lived on. It was also our playground when Mum and Dad weren't home. It was what I could only describe as a *family road*. To our left, there were the Smalls from Barbados. They had three girls and two boys and they owned the West Indian shop next to us which later became a hairdresser. Then on my right were the Husseins, who were a Turkish family. Further down you had the Fraters who were Jamaican/Indian, and then next to them were the Adams family who were from Barbados. Then in front of us, we had the Pascal family from St. Lucia. The Leeks lived around the corner, an English family.

Our road was a complete melting pot of cultures and we all got on very well. It's only when I grew up that I realised that Jamaicans normally had a problem with the small islands and the small islands had a problem with the Jamaicans. I didn't know anything about that in my childhood because we were all different—Asian, English, Jamaican, St. Lucian, Bajan, Trinidadian—we were all great neighbours, always inside each others' homes.

My best friend Joy lived next door and my mate Janet on the other side, with Elizabeth behind. As I got slightly older, we would always be out on the street at night, sitting and talking. Our parents would have to come out and say, "Come on, inside now."

We would reply with typical teen frustration: "God! It's only twelve o'clock!" This happened mostly in the holidays when we'd have our go-carts and we'd be playing conkers. That whole childhood thing.

Hilly Fields Park was just around the corner. It was the park to be at. We had the best times there, we practically lived there, and if that wasn't enough, in the evenings we would have games at the park; the community would come out to play rounders, box hockey, and football.

Where I grew up, every road has a memory; if it wasn't the friends that you remembered, it was the incidents, the fights, the romance. The boys you'd fancied, how you'd walk slowly past their house and smile your best smile in your old house clothes because you couldn't dress up to go outside in your Sunday best, you must be mad, that there is reserved for Jesus! You had to wear clothes that could be thrown away tomorrow; you had to have clothes that could get torn, dirty, and roomy enough so you could run at any given moment. Knock Down Ginger was the testing game to see if you had it. It was a random game that could take place at any given time. Whoever was bored at that particular moment would sneak into someone's garden without warning, ring a stranger's bell, and, without missing a beat, scream, "Run!"

You didn't need to turn back, it was never taken for granted that there was nothing to run for, you didn't turn around to see if it was a false alarm. You scarpered down the road, only slowing down when there was enough distance between you and the house and the owner standing outside shouting. You'd look back, knowing you were safe. The sweat pouring down your face, the panting, the laughter, and the fear of being caught all mixed up in your emotions. Then someone would shout to run again. *'Wait a minute'*, I'd think, *'I haven't got my breath back!'* But you had to run.

I remember the alley from Sandrock Road; many a breathing break was taken there. Sometimes you'd get a really terrible neighbour who wouldn't give up running after you; they'd run, screaming and shouting, not giving up. We'd slowly jog in front of them, we knew the street, and we could jump behind the houses up the alley behind Overcliff Road and be in the park in minutes playing like good little children. The times you were on your own were the scary times because you'd see the people you'd been terrorising when you were in your gang but now you were on your own. Still, your standby 'Run!' button was always ready to go.

Summer was pretty much Hilly Fields Park every day. My brothers would play football and Michael would check on me now and again. I was usually playing rounders. But he had to make sure nothing happened to me or he'd have to explain to my parents and that would not be nice.

We were no angels but we weren't out to harm each other; that thought just wasn't in us. We never took it too far, we didn't have any hate in our hearts for each other, we were truly just children being children. Sometimes there would be fights with kids from other roads nearby because they threw eggs at our window. Then we'd plot on how to get them back. It was a long way from the gun or knife crime we see today. Back then, it was egg crime! *'We're going to come down when you're sleeping; we're going to throw eggs at your window.'* Then, if we saw that person the very next day and we were all by ourselves, we'd say "Alright?" and be like best friends.

My road was special. We'd jump over fences to get to each other's houses and the house we were in changed daily. Who was not talking to who wouldn't last long, we would all make it up by the end of the day. When we went in to have a bath, we were dirty. We'd earned our filth! There were no computer games so we never spent the day just sitting still. We went to bed sweating. I remember my mum would come into our bedroom and say, "Angela, get in the bath, you're a mess, dirty and sweaty."

I think that is what childhood is about.

There was an apple tree in my next-door neighbour's garden and Mrs Hussein used to say to us, "You can have it, you can take the apples. If you want apples, take the apples."

"Alright then," we replied in unison, "we'll take the apples." We'd take the apples and I'd boil them up and make apple crumble and I'd charge 15 pence for a slice to the kids around the area.

Michael was always business-minded, he completely approved of me turning this innocent apple tree into a huge business deal as long as I washed up after myself. I made sure the kitchen was clean before my mother got home. If it wasn't, it would be Michael who would get in trouble. Looking back, I don't know why we didn't use this opportunity to get him into trouble… Perhaps we were too scared of the repercussions.

Every summer holiday, Philip Small, who lived next door and was rather fond of my apple crumble, would ask me, "Angela, when are you going to make some apple crumble?"

"Okay," I'd reply. This could turn into a little business. I thought, '*This apple crumble thing tastes nice, and it's so easy to make. All it takes is a bit of sugar, butter and flour, mix it in, oven, 15 pence a slice, I'm loaded.*'

So I would do that throughout the summer holidays until we ran out of apples. It'd be like, "Where are all the apples? Hurry up and grow, you little one up there!"

Chapter 6:
Home alone

When Mum and Dad went to work, Larry and I were left with Mrs Pascal, our childminder who lived opposite us in a massive house that took up the space of two houses. The family came from St. Lucia. Mrs Pascal had a little sing-song in her voice, she was larger than life and she looked like the woman in the *Tom and Jerry* cartoons, the one who wore an apron and held a rolling pin. We only ever saw that cartoon woman's legs.

No matter what time of day it was, Mrs Pascal's house always smelled of spaghetti and mashed potatoes. It was a warm smell. Even when my mum used to make it, I'd eat it and think it felt warm inside. It made me feel small and safe, like a baby.

Mum had to work, there was no more staying at home with us. Every morning when my mum was working and it was time for the childminder, Larry and I would go over there, we'd sit down and just be. It was almost like we sat down and behaved, we didn't do anything. We just sat there, behaving ourselves. That was the strict instruction: "Behave!" It's like we waited for the day to go by and while we waited, we had something to eat.

When we didn't go to Mrs Pascal's, we looked forward to going back because we knew we would get that special dish. It's a dish that makes you feel warm inside, you felt safe, we were going to sit there and wait, wait to be looked after, and that meant spaghetti and mashed potatoes. This was no ordinary dish; this meal was cooked with love and attention. This woman loved us; she wanted our tummies to be happy.

When my mum used to pop out to go shopping, a trip that wasn't enough to justify our going to the babysitter, Mum would leave us in her room with a Tango drink and chicken flavour Golden Wonder crisps. She'd leave the food and the radio on. The radio was a cream-coloured wireless with a green leather band all the way around. My dad had fixed that radio until it was unfixable! It was so old. The batteries were chipped and held in place by a piece of Sellotape. Dad just wanted to keep this radio alive.

The radio was tuned to the London station LBC. Mum would leave LBC on and go to Lewisham shopping or on some other errand. Today this wouldn't be acceptable; Mum would probably be arrested and social services would be on the line. But because she gave us what we needed and just shut the door, we knew to stay there and be quiet.

We didn't dare leave the room. We stayed in their bedroom alone and wouldn't go wandering downstairs for anything. Mum said not to move so we didn't. She made sure we had a glass of water or juice and some snacks or sandwiches set out for us along with bathroom access so we didn't need to leave the room. We savoured the sweetness of the Tango and the crisps while we listened to the news.

Why the news, why LBC? I must have been hooked on LBC by the time I was eight or nine years old. I made my first radio appearance as a child. I told a joke on LBC. I phoned the show that they had on in the mornings called *Jelly Bones*, which I listened to every week until I plucked up enough courage to call in. When I eventually got through, they asked who I was.

"Angela."

"You have a joke for us, Angela, go ahead," the presenter said.

"Knock knock."

"Who's there?" replied the host, playing along.

"Annette."

"Annette who?" he asked, just as I was expecting.

"Annette is good for fishing!" I put down the phone in triumph.

I shouted to Larry, "Did you not hear me, did you hear me, did you hear me?" I was so excited. It was like, "Oh God, I was on the radio!"

Sometimes I can't believe that I called the radio at the age of eight or nine. Maybe I'd been listening to LBC for such a long time that subconsciously I felt a relationship with it as natural as the relationship with my brother. If I could tell a joke to Larry and make him laugh, I could tell my joke to my friends on the radio too.

Chapter 7:
Blackout

From a very young age, I spent a lot of my time thinking. I would think until I had a headache. I made sure there were always paracetamol or other tablets around because I didn't like the idea of having headaches. I would think about everything people said and rewrote their dialogue in my head, putting a spin on it.

If only they knew how that would be funny if they did this and that happened. Scenes flashed through my mind as I laughed inside. At home, I could share my funny ideas with my dad and with my brothers. I would tell a story like, "Dad, this happened…" and it would be funny.

Dad would always frown and reply, "You silly girl." I'd be thinking, '*Would you laugh please, Daddy? Laugh, it's funny*'. He would smile at my need to hear the laugh, but the smile was too quiet; if I turned around, I wouldn't know if he'd found it funny. Laugh out loud, make it known to me please; a chuckle will do until you make a louder sound. I had no idea the responsibility was on me.

When I heard my dad laughing, what a feeling that was! He was funny too and I laughed at most of what he said. He had a dry sense of humour, perfect timing. So when he laughed at my jokes, I could bow, I knew that meant it was great because he wasn't one to burst out laughing, and instead he'd just comment, "You silly girl" which clearly meant, *'Try harder, I'm not just going to give it to you.'* Great training, I guess.

My brothers used to be more enthusiastic, "Do that thing when you pretend to be Mummy, Angie."

I would stand in front of the TV, especially when we had candles back in the day when we were experiencing one of those regular blackouts. We'd always have candles out and I would always be talking, making faces, using my fingers and hands casting characters on the wall with the shadows.

This was the time to shine; no one else wanted that stage. I would jump at the chance to stand up in front of my family, act out all the voices, my parents' Jamaican accent. I played out their conversations. I'd quote their sayings: "New broom sweep clean, but old broom knows corners." "Duppy know who fi frighten".

We had blackouts once a week and at the moment the lights went out, I would think, *"Oh, we've got a blackout, wicked."* Once the lights were out, we would all gather in the dining room and then we'd sit there together, waiting patiently for the lights to come back on. Sometimes it would be quick and we'd talk for only a short while. Other times, though, it would be so long, so we needed to have some entertainment, and that's when the wall would come alive.

We would light the candles and laugh and joke together. Probably my parents intended this to dispel any childish fear of the dark. It was quite an intimate moment really because we had to stay there as a family without any distractions, all in one place. We had to talk; it's not a time for bad vibes. So we would share our stories, jokes, and laughter.

Mum would talk about Jamaica and Dad would talk about his childhood adventures. "This reminds me of a time when we were in May Pen…" he would explain. Everybody had a story to tell and nobody wanted to leave the room.

There was no getting in trouble in this place of darkness with a little bit of light. I looked forward to blackouts because I could reflect and express, "Oh, blackout, blackout, blackout, wooo…wooo…wooo…" I'd be a ghost, and my brothers would say, "Oh, shut up, Angie, here she goes again."

I would tap secretly on the table making ghostly noises and Larry would protest, "Mum, she's doing that!"

I'm like, "What?" while tapping secretly under the table.

I remember sitting there knowing I was wetting myself and thinking, *'I'm wetting myself but I'd rather not to go toilet.'* I would risk peeing rather than miss one of Dad's stories and if push came to shove, I could act as though it had been an accident. Eventually, I would be bursting. "I've got to go to the toilet, can somebody please come with me? I can't hold it anymore." Rohan would usually be the one to come with me.

"Come on, Angie."

"Thanks, Teddy." That was his pet name, Teddy. We would run upstairs and he'd be very loyal and wait at the top of the stairs. I would wash my hands and come back down and it would be alright.

But with my other brothers, there was no way it would be alright. You couldn't ask Michael because Michael didn't do toilet trips. Larry would take me but leave me when I was still using the toilet. I remember many times I'd wet myself jumping off the toilet because he ran off. He would end up outside yelling back at me, "Hurry up!"

"Wait, I'm not finished yet."

"Hurry up, I'm going now." And then he'd run down the stairs and I would just leave the toilet and run down the stairs because the idea of being upstairs by myself was terrifying—it's almost like I created something to scare myself.

If Larry was going to the toilet, I'd do the same to him. I'd be outside the door going, "Oh my God, Larry, there's something up here with us, I'm scared, I'm going…see you later."

We just did it to each other and neither of us seemed to wise up to the fact that we were mucking about. We needed each other because downstairs seemed so far away. I needed company even if it was only Larry who was just as terrified as me.

Sometimes my parents would send us upstairs for something, "Go upstairs and look on my dressing table for this thing."

I'd think, "No, this is the haunted house, I can't go…"

It wasn't a haunted house; we created it in our heads. I was always scared to go upstairs by myself. When I used to do those little visits with my brother and wind him up, I was setting myself up because I scared myself more than him!

In longer blackouts, Mum would make little treats and serve us by candlelight. There was a dish that she would make; it was salt fish with tomato, made with a little bit of oil and pepper. She'd mix it all together and it would taste like heaven. Mixed with bread and served with Mum's cup of tea, this was enough for us all to feel happy and full. "We've got salt fish and tomatoes," we would say, salivating. For me, salt fish was good-time food. That food still sends me back to childhood.

She made it for us in Jamaica a couple of years ago and I was like, "God, that feeling is so warm."

Chapter 8:
Hit him!

"It's alright for you, you've got brothers," my friends wouldn't tire of telling me. They were right. I knew whatever happened in life, I've got brothers, so I'm pretty much going to be okay. Having brothers is like having full-time security; they give you a very safe feeling. You can walk into any situation and cause a problem because you have got brothers. You could play happily in the playground at school and not be picked on because everyone had received the press release, 'Angie has brothers, do not touch!'

I think my behaviour was just a little over the top. I really made the most of my brothers: girls loved me because they fancied one of them so they needed me, and I guess I needed sweets. My brothers were in demand from the girls and played games. As I had information that could be detrimental to their cause, I found another way of making extra pocket money. It would cost them to keep my mouth from saying, "He's got another girlfriend." This was very profitable, but when they were single, I was skint.

One Sunday afternoon, there was an incident on the street outside. Some boys pushed me and spat at me, but it shocked me to realise that my brothers weren't there when I needed them. It was a brother moment. I couldn't take those boys on alone.

I went inside and called out to all three of them. Michael came out, Rohan came out, Larry came out, and I went to show them the boys. I remember Michael was really angry which surprised me because he was so strict at home and was always telling me off and pinching me, and if I did anything wrong, he'd say, "You. Upstairs," and that was that.

I'd think, "Oh God, I'm going to get hit when I get upstairs." I would watch television thinking, *'Oh, it's alright for you and the world, but I'm going to get beaten when I get upstairs because I've upset my brother.'* I would say, "It was Michael who did it, Mum."

So when Michael came out to handle these boys, I thought, *'God, he cares'* because he was really angry.

"You did what to my sister; you did what?"

Rohan was right behind him and Larry was right behind Rohan. So we went around the corner and my brothers called them out and said, "Look, what's this that you did to my sister?"

I was all confident. "That's right, you did do that, yes, you did do that. Don't pull out of it now, not because we've got this crowd here. You said that and you spat at me, yes you did, you did, I wouldn't make it up."

It was the cockiest confidence because the thing is they did do it, and I didn't understand why they would deny it…until I looked at my brothers! I think now, of course, that you're supposed to deny it, you're damn right you didn't do it, save yourself. But at the time, I was shocked.

"No, of course, you did."

Then Michael said to me, "Hit him."

At the time, I thought, *'Don't be silly, I don't do this, you do this, this is why I called you. If I could have hit him at the time, I would have hit him at the time; this is a brothers' moment…'*

Michael said, "Hit him."

I thought, *'No, I can't hit him, I can't hit someone who I know can't hit me back, that's unfair.'* Yet I still knew I had to hit him because my brother had told me to. He couldn't hit back and it gave me a very uncomfortable feeling, especially with people watching. I hit him hard on the chest and then my brothers shouted, "Hit him again!"

I started to get confident; I was like, "Take it if you can." It became one of those 'thump, bam, bam" chest moments. He shouted, "No!"

"Yeah... Whatever... You're going to learn," I replied.

I was hitting and hitting and hitting, and then I stopped and looked at what I had done to the person who had pushed me and realised, "Alright, I've finished."

Then Michael said into my ear, "When we're not there, because we're not always going to be there, that's how you have to do it. You can't always call on your brothers to come and fight your wars; there's going to be a time when we won't be there, Angie, and I want you to remember that's how you handled it."

Oh, talk about a lesson! *'That was a heavy moment,'* I thought.

"Yeah, okay, can I walk with you guys on the way back?" I replied.

I felt confident. I think there's a confidence you feel, like if you know you've got money, there's a way you feel when you want something—you don't really want it but you know you've got the money for it. It was the same thing with my brothers. Having the confidence of my brothers behind me, I knew that at any given time I could call on them, but I didn't want to use them again.

I've never really called them for anything else in my life like that. And one of the reasons for that is because of the way they are—Rohan especially is a nutter! So I would be putting him in trouble. If there was a situation, he would take it to the extreme, and I'd think, *'Now you're going to prison, so that was pointless.'*

So I knew that I would never call upon my brothers again because they would go all out to protect me and that scared me. But the confidence of knowing they were there made me not need them again anyway. But you know what? I figured it out that I can handle these types of situations all by myself. I think it's in the eyes.

That lesson from my brothers was a turning point and I knew that I'd got to learn how to manage this myself because they wouldn't always be there. I don't think they realised what they were doing. Maybe they did, maybe Michael knew what he was doing because Michael's a very psychologically savvy person.

If he said to me, "No, you can't do so-and-so," I would immediately want to do it. He's the sort of brother who'll say, "You can't do that, you can't do stand-up."

"Yes, I can."

"Yeah, well show us then."

"Alright, I'll show you."

And I did, and he was delighted.

My relationship with Michael's always been a proving one. Even as an adult when I write plays, every script I write has a 'Michael' in it. It was only when the friend who types up my scripts said to me, "No doubt there's a Michael in there" that I noticed.

I hadn't realised and when I questioned what she'd just said, she replied, "Angie, every time you've written a sketch or a play or whatever, there's a character called Michael in it."

So I looked at this new script and thought, '*God, there is a Michael.*'

It's like this Michael character is always in whatever I do; there's always a Michael. Michael is the brother that can do everything. When Michael said to me, "If you can conceive it, you can achieve it," I said, "Really?" But I believed him. I set my expectations high because if I can conceive high goals, and that means I've got to go and achieve them.

Little did I know that when I went to school, everything would change and I would need my brother's advice more than ever.

Chapter 9
Black girls don't run

We'd stand there waiting, waiting for this so-called game Kiss Chase to start. The whistle would blow, the sound of freedom, and we would charge out to the playground. It's not like we were looking for a relationship at eight years old, it was just the game we played. But we little blacks girls wore our plimsolls for no reason; when we ran that way, all the boys, including the little black boys, ran in the opposite direction. We needed to work out why they ran away from us.

Our hair was beautifully combed and plaited into lovely square boxes, red and blue polka dot ribbons wove through the stylish plaits, the smell of La India or Dixie Peach Hair oil followed us through the school like a close friend. Our skin was shining, our clothes stiff from the starched ironing early that morning, white ankle socks in our shiny polished shoes. We were at our best, but still they refused to run after us. We would look at the boys running after the hair that seemed to move in the wind, bouncing and flowing, the little white girls, their cheeks rosy with laughter as they ran at speed because all the boys wanted them, even ours. We didn't have to run; we'd look silly running without a cause, so we stood in the playground, praying for this game to end.

We didn't have a diversity department at the school; we couldn't go in and complain about the lack of kisses or demand that another game must be played, one that included all of us.

We walked home from school looking at our little brothers, wondering why they couldn't have made us feel a little bit pretty by kissing us. *'Couldn't you just pretend?'* Now we were going to take this lesson into our lives, disappointed and hurt. Brian Curlu eventually kissed me, but it was on the way home, not in public. I was standing still, he never chased me. But I still loved him for it, a child's kind of love.

I have some fond memories of the formative years of my school life. I remember my teacher, Mr Woodgate. I went to Lewisham Bridge Primary School. I was about eight years old and Mr Woodgate was the teacher that I fell in love with. There's always one teacher in a child's life that you can point out and that special teacher for me was Mr Woodgate. He was a white man with a really thick beard and long thick hair that came down to his shoulders. He wore glasses, and I remember thinking, *'I really love this teacher.'*

Looking back, I don't know why I fell in love with him; I think it's because he was a caring person. He taught drama at school and he always encouraged me. He put me in little plays and all the little school productions.

The students were allowed to get the teachers coffee and take it back to the classroom and wash the cup up and leave it on the side when they'd finished with it. This was considered somebody's duty and I remember my friend Sandra and I used to challenge each other to get that coffee and the mug so that one of us could wash it. We'd walk holding onto the teacher watching him sip the coffee slowly and sometimes he'd get a little bit of coffee on his moustache. I would stand there thinking, *'He's nearly finished; if I can get that cup, I will be teacher's pet.'* I found myself repeating my thoughts: *'I want to get that cup; I want to get that cup.'* I was obsessed with Mr Woodgate.

And every day, it was the same thing; Sandra and I would watch him like hawks. Sometimes she'd get the cup before me; sometimes I'd get the cup before her and I'd run with that cup and go wash it out. I really wanted his approval because he was such a nice teacher.

"Is there anything we can do for you, Sir?"

"Would you like us to do this?"

He was one of those teachers who made you think. Any child with a teacher like that right through their school years would end up a very intelligent happy person.

The x-factor about him was that he cared that you learned and he would share stories and he would talk to you and make you feel like you were somebody, and that was encouraging. He would tell us about his life; he'd just open up to us. He was married to Mrs Woodgate, who was also a teacher. We were scared of her and when we had her in the last two years, we were just broken children. It was like we wanted Mr Woodgate but we've got Mrs Woodgate instead.

Our last few years of primary school were so different to the years spent with Mr Woodgate. I'd fantasise about what his class was like and how happy those children were while he was teaching them and how they were laughing and basking in his presence. I'd remember the fun memories of the stories he'd be sharing. But this teacher, his wife, wasn't like that and we couldn't understand why they were married. I mean, she was the opposite of him.

Mr Woodgate left his mark on me. When I left primary school, I never found another teacher who measured up to him. You have so many teachers; one for Maths, English, Science, but in our primary school, only one was a unique teacher.

We used to measure teachers on the Woodgate scale: were they closer to Mr Woodgate or closer to Mrs Woodgate? Unfortunately, they were all like Mrs

Woodgate. He set the bar for me as far as ideal teachers go and it was a very high bar indeed. We *loved* him. Even when I think about him now, I wonder how he is, I wonder if he's still alive because really, he was a very good man. It's only when I had other teachers that I realised that most of them don't care and we're all just numbers to them. I felt that quite early on at school. I felt like they didn't even know if we were there.

I didn't know how to adjust to all the teachers in the big school and my big expectations and wanting to be intelligent made things even more difficult. I never felt very intelligent as a child. I only started to feel intelligent when I left school. When I was at school, I felt below average. I think it was mostly to do with my reading but everybody else seemed to know things and everybody else had experienced things.

When you're growing up in the black community, some of your white friends will go on holiday and come back and talk about where they went and they'd draw this part of the plane and they'd talk about going to Spain, whereas some of the black children would just say, "Well, I stayed at home." That was our holiday.

I tried to enjoy school but it was hard; it never excited me after Mr Woodgate.

Chapter 10:
Fighting with the words

I felt dumb; I felt stupid; I felt dumb and stupid every time I had to deal with the words. It was like I was going to war.

I had no issues around reading at primary school, I was too busy playing and having fun. It wasn't until much later on in life that I found out I was dyslexic—you'd think that a word like dyslexia would be easy to spell and say, to at least ease the burden on us. And it is a burden; I can only explain it like that. When you start to read, it's very difficult. For me, the words disappear at random. I start to read and it's like the whole sentence will just decide to get up and walk out the door, like, *'Now Angie needs us, let's just get up and run off the page, won't that be fun?'* And I think, *'What's going on? Where are they going? Excuse me! Not now, you're making a fool out of me...'*

Too late; I'm already feeling stupid.

Then just as you try once more, they disappear again and you can't stabilise it. I don't feel like doing it again because the words keep letting me down. You just want to shut it down. You don't want to see books. You don't want anybody to ask you to read aloud, you want to keep all that private, you and the page in silence, in a room, no one watching. I'm in awe when I watch someone reading fluently, I wonder, *'Wow, what are the words doing on your page? Please share with me what it is you are doing?'*

There's a slight resentment because that child or person has got something that you haven't got and as far as you're concerned, you're never going to get it. It's never going to work for you... There's a fit of anger, resentment, but my anger came out as humour. I'd tell jokes; I'd laugh at myself so if somebody noticed that I couldn't get a word right, I'd crack a joke and everybody would laugh.

The most haunting noise you can hear in a room before you're about to read is when everybody goes, "Ohhh..." Even to this day, that sound still haunts me.

It means they've heard and noticed my weakness and they think I'm pathetic, dumb, and they think I'm stupid. So that's really how I see words, and it was only when I was older, after I had gone to an audition, that I first heard the word dyslexia. Someone had finally worked it out for me. The director said, "You're dyslexic," after I'd struggled through the script.

I didn't understand; I thought that it was some disease. I played it over in my head, "Dyslexic? What are you talking about?"

So she said, "The way you read, you read as though you're fighting with the words."

I wanted to tell her, yes; we have been at war since I was a little girl, but it's a war I'm never going to win, so I've accepted, well...I just don't read very well. But I'm here now because I want this role.

The audition was stressful. I remember just deciding to go for it. I wasn't doing well; in fact, I was really bad. It was so embarrassing that I'd gone for this audition where my friends had already got through and it was just me left, and they were hoping, wishing and praying I'd get a role too. I went into this audition, fingers crossed, thinking, *'I've got to get this role,'* because it meant I would go to Switzerland with this group and my two best friends have gone through, so I had to get in too. When I started auditioning, it was a real mess. I was staggering, I was sweating, the words were disappearing, they weren't coming back, they didn't care. I was terrible, but I got to the end, and the director said to me, "It wasn't a good audition, you know that, don't you?" Talk about keeping it real!

I was just about to walk out because I thought I'd made a fool of myself when she said, "It wasn't the audition, it was the fact that you finished, and that's what I'm going to employ." I couldn't believe it; I just thought, 'Wow!'

That's how I got the role. I finished it, I didn't give up. I never forgot that, and even today I say Dad's words to people, 'Whatever you start, finish, because somebody's looking to see if you have the guts to get to the end even when it's all going against you'. You stand there and you finish, someone will give you the role.

She said, "You're going to learn the words anyway, you're never going to have to read the lines because you can learn the words. As an actor, you'll be fine, but your strength isn't in auditioning, your strength is elsewhere, so I'm going to give you the role." The joy I felt! And I never let go of how she released the worry in me.

It made sense; I have this thing, this difficult condition with the difficult name. So? Am I someone who can function in the world with this thing? Does this dyslexia disease explain my behaviour at school? But how can it? It's just words, words that seem to make my life hell. Those words are going to get me. When I'm feeling comfortable and having a laugh, something will need to be read aloud, and that's when they strike.

'Look, everyone, the little funny girl who you are all adoring, well let me show you something about her, you won't notice it until you give her this book... Read aloud, girl!' Sweat starts to gather up for the great outpouring, nerves are set to go, and the words get ready to dance, like they're in a funky rave, up, down, across, sideways, wait for it, and spin! Once the words have settled back down, it's too late to salvage my pride, it's too late, they all know she can't read!

I just had to get through it. I had tests; yep, you are severely dyslexic.

"What can I do?"

"Nothing at this stage."

"What about my life? My career is dependent on me being able to read, especially aloud. Can I take a tablet? Is there any medical treatment?"

"No, you are just going to have to manage and think outside the box. See it as a gift and look for the positive side. Failing that, blue and yellow paper can help to stabilise the words."

"Oh, okay, thanks."

Note to self: get all my books printed on blue paper.

Chapter 11:
Jumping jacks

We had trampolines in our gym at school and one day I realised that this would be the ideal place to hide if we didn't go to our lessons. The lessons were so boring, I couldn't concentrate, the teachers had no excitement about them... I needed a little bit of fun. The thought of biology, then history, followed by maths—was God punishing me for something? Why were we here?

Yes, I knew we were there to learn, I got that. But couldn't the teachers make more of an effort? Couldn't they use colours and background music to get us in the mood for learning? And while we're talking about it, can we get a new design for these uniforms? Why must we all dress the same? You teachers don't.

Mr Benson had it in for me; why, I don't know...yes I do, I was annoying. If he said something, I would always crack a joke. Really I was just trying to stop the class so I didn't have to be bored. It was the least I could do, for me. I didn't really appreciate that I was being a distraction.

There were some lessons that weren't valuable to me so I thought there was no need to go, especially as there were other pressing things to do. Once I'd worked out how to miss a class, I had to put it into practice, that's what training is all about.

My friends Georgina and Jackie and I sneaked out of class and went downstairs to the sports hall. We loved the trampolines; in fact, we couldn't get enough, the sports lessons were too short; why couldn't we just bounce all day? These were the lessons that needed extending, not double RE! I already went to church so I should have got a pass.

We needed to do something; as friends, we were on the same page. Let's do this! We didn't need encouragement and we weren't stupid enough to have a well-behaved friend who might make us see reason about going to our lessons. We were going to hop our lessons, no, not the same as truant, no, because that means you didn't come to school, we would never do that. To hop is to hop over a lesson and then grace the next lesson with your presence.

So we got down to the gym, spotted the big bouncer and that was it, we jumped on it. We had a lookout to watch for those gym teachers (they can be so aggressive), and we didn't need anyone messing with our new-found focused energy. We stayed on the trampoline and jumped and jumped and jumped. And then somebody shouted out, "Marriott's coming! Marriott's coming!" We could now die.

That's Mrs Marriott; of all the sports teachers, why her? Marriot didn't mess around, who knows if she even liked children? She was only working as a teacher to pay her rent or look after her mother, or maybe she was just a good sports teacher. I was already up high on the trampoline and I couldn't get off easily so I just jumped straight off and broke my ankle. That was the effect of hearing "Marriott's coming", pain was the option; I didn't even think about my safety. Marriot was here and I had to get out. So I went to hospital.

I could have died or been left paralysed, but that had no bearing on the fact that I should have been in my lesson.

Suspended, how could they? I didn't know how to break it to my family. I was creating history in my family, my first suspension. Could we look at this in a positive way, see it as pioneering? The first to…it may not be Harriet Tubman or Rosa Parks, but it is me. So that was the first suspension and my mum realised. *'Wait a minute, not only did you get suspended, but you've come home with a broken ankle?'*

Going back to school was difficult. The time that I'd missed affected me and I felt disconnected again; it was almost as though I couldn't catch up, but then again I wasn't trying. I wasn't enjoying this school and it was worse than just being bored; my head didn't go at the same pace, I didn't process as quickly, I'd get the right answers but not at the same time as the rest of the class. This made me feel lost. I would reason in my head and come up with the right answers, or in the discussions I'd draw the same conclusions as the bright ones in the class, but because I never said it out loud, as far as the teacher was concerned I didn't know. After we'd finished a class, the same teacher now wanted me to go home, in my playtime, my television time, and do homework. Were these people insane? Did they know how much playing I could do in three hours, especially in the summer? *'Alright, I'll do a bit, but no promises.'*

Of course, I fell behind. I didn't want to catch up. Then the disruptive behaviour started to kick in, I was always on report, always getting told off, always being chucked out of class and sent to the Headmistress' office. All the teachers would pass me by and say, "It's you again, Angela. Why are you here again?"

I'm waiting there and, oh no, here she comes, walking down the corridor; we always knew it was her, her heels hammered invisible nails into the ground. She walked like she owned the school, the books that she was clutching suffocating her breasts, the same breasts that were trying to break out of her dress—they wanted to get away too. Every time my house mistress Mrs Kiddle saw me, she would give me that look that said, "What's the point, Angela?" She would look over her glasses and wonder what she was going to do with me this time. I would get even more annoyed when the teachers assumed I was doomed, doomed because their lessons were boring, dumb and uninspiring for me. How come they didn't get the blame for not keeping Angela interested?

I would think, *'I've been sent by God, didn't you know that? I'm just going to misbehave in my lessons; surely that's what you all want. I'm sorry if it ruins your class. Honestly, that was not my aim, I was just bored.'*

Secondary school is where you find your first real best friends, and my best friend was Yvonne Williams. To this day, no one can laugh like Yvonne. We were a team, speaking backslang and being on report together. We would miss school and go to her house and make cheese and pickle sandwiches. We were proper gangster: we learned how to squeeze the juice from the pickle while it was still in the jar using only a knife! We lived in the fast lane.

Georgia was a part of the team. We would meet every morning to get up to our little antics, visiting our local sweet shop. Georgia and I lived opposite, a road apart. We were in each other's houses day and night; we were double best friends, friends at school and then friends at home. At school, we'd part for a bit then walk back together to continue the home friendship. We knew each other inside out. It was a very protective friendship; we defended each other to the end. We could get beaten by our parents in front of each other and that was it, our secret.

Mr Benson was my form teacher. I think having myself and Yvonne in the class was too much for him. I was awful to him. I had fun with Sir; I could wind him up because he was a young teacher so it was like a game to me. I gave that man hell, so much so that when I saw him years later as an adult, I apologised to him. I said, "Sir, I must apologise for my behaviour at school."

He said, "No problem. I am so proud of you! I tell everyone I taught Angie Le Mar."

Halfway through secondary school, I left after getting suspended. I'd been suspended so many times that now it was time to leave. After the expulsion, I was supposed to go to another school, but at the time I couldn't get into one because they didn't want me. They said I was too disruptive.

And what about my friend Yvonne? Who would she laugh with? I still see my friend from school, every time as strong as yesterday, solid to this day.

Chapter 12:
The disconnection

I spent six months at home and my mum kept giving me cleaning and cooking and washing to do because I couldn't just sit there.

I knew it wasn't going to be plain-sailing. I knew my mum would find things for me to do, but I thought it might be a little maths here and there, a little story writing, masquerading as an English teacher, work that would have been hard for her but easy for me. Nope, no schoolwork; no get your books here. It was just, grab that basin, I want you to wash down this wall. Next, I need you to scrub the skirting boards, before you iron these clothes.

But what about my education! I never believed I would wish to be at school. I actually missed getting into trouble, I missed my friends. It slowly dawned on me what this school experience truly meant to me.

It was a very difficult time because I realised how important school was, not just the lessons or the education, but the friends. I had no contact with my friends. We didn't have Facebook or Twitter; there was nothing. Just a few accidental meetings on the high street. I was completely cut off from everyone. They thought I was coming back but I knew I wasn't going back to that school, I knew it was over. I'd gone too far this time. Plus I had cleaning to be getting on with.

I think my mother knew I couldn't stay at home, apart from the fact that it was illegal, I had my rights to learn, my people had fought for me to learn and she knew that.

So I needed to go to a new school, we were all decided on that. Well it didn't go as easily as I thought it might have…no school in the borough wanted me to go to their school… You've got to be kidding, why not? A few disruptive moments and the schools are saying no? We had a fight on our hands, and fight we did. We had to speak with the Education Authority, we were sent to meetings at the Racial Equality Unit; we met with Sybil Phoenix and Baroness Ros Howells, who I still know to this day.

Back then, these ladies fought for me to get into a school. Obstacles were about to be knocked down, these women were not giving up. I was so in awe of them, they were real powerhouses. When they gave us the news that I had been accepted into a new school, I nearly cried!

So, I was now a new member of Blackheath Bluecoat School after leaving Lewisham Girls. I joined in the third year, which is a hard year for you to start another school as the pupils have already got used to each other and friendships have been formed.

I felt I was going to struggle in this new school if I didn't get into the right group. I couldn't be a pushover. I had to go in there quite confident or I'd be picked on. But if I wanted to fit in, I couldn't stick out like a sore thumb… It was hard starting a new school for the second time. I'd already done the new secondary school bit, and here I was again. And this time, I knew I had to make it work.

I found friends quickly. I knew the odd faces from church, but I needed to find the group that no one messed with. It was easy to spot. You know the ones; they were the sort of girls who were loud in and out of class, the ones who didn't go to lessons on time. I found them. Now I had to prove myself to them.

I made things seem bigger than they really were: "Yeah, I got kicked out of another school." This always gives you a bit of credibility. "Yes, I'm from Lewisham Girls School, not the best reputation when it comes to schools. Yep, I'm from there, in fact, I was kicked out for there." Somehow I managed to take my complete self there too. It wasn't long before the jokes came rushing out, I was the funny one and the one that could fight if push came to shove.

The Deputy Head was called Miss Cross and I thought it was her nickname because she was always cross, always miserable and a nightmare. She was one of those teachers who could handle you, she wasn't scared. I know you need teachers like that but she made my life a little difficult.

It was less than a year in when I got into trouble, suspended again. It wasn't my fault I got suspended. I tried to explain that to my worn-out mother. No, it wasn't my fault. It was because of that film *10* with Bo Derek. She had her hair in cornrows and everybody wanted that famous hairdo. They all thought that cornrows just started because Bo Derek had her hair styled like that. The white girls at school could wear cornrows and put beads in, but the black girls couldn't. It wasn't as big as the Martin Luther King movement, but it was a start. We decided that we would stand in the playground, put some hand cream on our foreheads and chant, "huckleday, huckleday, huckleday."

No one knew what "huckleday" was. I know I didn't know what "huckleday" was and I was the one who'd made it up. But we stood in the playground and we said we're going to stand here and we are all going to chant and we are going to make sure we get our rights today to wear our beads and cornrows. There were about six or seven of us and we stood there chanting, "huckleday, huckleday, huckleday."

Miss Cross was having none of this, so she and the other teachers started to intimidate us. One of us would be summoned away and then the next would disappear and then it was down to Debbie and me. We just looked at each other chanting, "huckleday, huckleday, huckleday" and, needless to say, we got suspended. But they did allow us to wear beads in our hair after that so I felt like I was an activist from an early age.

But I still had to explain this to my mum. She got right to the point while telling me off and said, "You don't even wear beads!"

I just knew that I had to fight for it. I kept thinking, *'How can it be right for you to do it when we can't do it? When I do it, it's a political statement but when you do it, it's just fashion.'* Something was wrong with that picture.

That was something that stuck with me. You can call me a troublemaker—maybe my intention was to be a troublemaker—but it turned out that it was political at the end of it. My mum couldn't understand it because I didn't wear beads or put my hair in cornrows. As far as she was concerned, I'd been suspended for nothing.

She didn't understand that it was the principle of the thing. And at the time, this whole situation felt so wrong. So I stood by my actions and then I got into trouble for it. When I returned to school, I was back on report. So now, as a result, I had to behave myself, but I can't behave myself, that's the thing. It's just not who I am.

Chapter 13:
Keep cracking those jokes

I was always bored at school. I didn't enjoy the lessons and the teachers didn't enjoy me. I got through most of my schooling by cracking jokes. Drama captured my heart though. My parents were just glad to see that I was doing well in something. They were so worried, it was hard for them to work out what I was going to become. I knew I was going to make people laugh; all my drama teachers got it too, they all saw it. I was always up for a role.

Drama teachers are so special, they have an ability to connect the English lesson to the art and see those who are having difficulties. It's as though they connect the dots.

But I still couldn't help myself. In the silence of a class, when everyone is being so well-behaved, it always seemed like the perfect opportunity to break into jokes…

So would Vauxhall College save me? This college was built for me; there were no rules, you don't go to lessons at your own peril. There were no teachers on my back, no one cared if I didn't take it seriously; you'd just be politely asked to leave, no meeting, no marching, just go!

This was a college, but with a difference: everyone here was having some kind of fun, good friends, good music; it was like having a sound system in the common room. At lunch breaks, you'd have a dance across the road in the local community centre. I'm not talking about a few disco lights, I'm talking about blacking out the windows, no light allowed through. This was to be a scrubbing session, this was where you'd dance closely with the person you fancied, and there were a lot of good-looking boys at college so you wouldn't do too badly.

You'd have your dance then you'd walk out of the darkness into the broad daylight, sunglasses on to help your eyes adjust.

We knew what we were doing, we were having a different kind of fun, we were getting close at midday, and we were forming relationships. We had crossed the line of learning. This was a new class, a class that could end up in a risky place; the lovers' rock music was too much, and we couldn't resist it. Afterwards you'd make your way to your lesson with your mind full of dancing. I'd think of memories of the dances we just had, and how wonderful it was.

My jokes at college were just getting sharper; I had to use all I had. I had most of my friends in stitches, all day every day.

We formed a posse, the SACI Posse: Shirleen, Angie, Cecila and Irene. We even got T-shirts and sweatshirts made, we planned our uniforms each day, we took our positions really seriously. We even had a little rap: "the SACI Posse is well wossi…" No idea what wossi was, but we were known.

The teachers didn't care if you weren't paying attention, they knew you would feel it soon. When you were sitting in the examination room, the jokes wouldn't be coming as fast and quickly as they usually did.

It was all making sense to me at last, this education thing was serious. I was going to need this later. I had got some catching up to do, I had some friends' books to borrow, and I had some late nights ahead of me.

I needed to connect with the teachers, the same ones who wanted me out of their classes so they could teach the children who wanted to learn. I tried to be humble and kind, but once it's gone, it's gone. I was going to have to get the next train, and this time pay attention.

Chapter 14:
The church girl

Church for me is part of who I am, where I'm coming from. When I attended church as a child, I never had an understanding of what church was. I had just the one understanding about church in those days and that was how to get out of it. It was far too boring for me and I had to go, there was no choice in the matter: it's what we do in our house, we go to church!

All I knew about church was that I couldn't do anything, it was my life. They made God feel like He was somebody who was going to punish you.

On Sunday mornings, no sickness was going to get you off church; my parents had heard every trick in the book, which were also often used for school too. By Sunday, you were out of excuses and you might need that one for school on Monday morning.

Sunday mornings started off with the sound of Jim Reeves playing downstairs. He was flying away…again! Then there would be the sweet smell of plantains being fried and Sunday dinner being semi-cooked, which meant you wouldn't have to cook for so long when you got back from church, starving.

Time to get up, get ready, and go to church… I was at that age where I still had to go but my older brothers were free to stay at home now. I had to put on my Sunday best and fix my natural hair into a style that would only ever last as far as the front door, then it would quit; even the hairstyle was getting fed up of going to church.

I would sometimes let my parents go ahead and I would walk; this would help control how long I had to stay in church, especially if I got there late because of all the people I was helping along the way. Can't argue with that.

We worshipped God; we prayed to God, but I didn't really understand. All I knew was I didn't know anything else, it was normal. My mum had got me here and my dad was convinced that he should be here too. So I just sat in the church killing time thinking, *'How do I get out of this?'*

I felt trapped. We couldn't do anything: we couldn't wear lipstick, we couldn't wear trousers, we couldn't straighten our hair, and we definitely couldn't have boyfriends. We couldn't do anything and I would often wonder how I'd ever survive this life that I was stuck inside.

My mum was raised in the church from a very young age, so the church and Christian life has always been her life and she wanted it to be our lives too.

So it was all about going to church and preaching and listening to people preaching. Don't get me wrong, there were great occasions when church was the place to be. This was because of your friends: we made the best friends at church; we spent some really good times together. There were different types of relationships, you had the really spiritual ones who you knew were going to stay in the church, come what may. Then you had the ones who were Christians now and again, depending on the powerful message that day.

We all had our reasons for going there, but, like my best friend Pamela Donaldson, I was going because I had to. We used to sit in church and laugh, everything was funny, we'd share sweets together, and we went to each other's house afterwards. Each summer holiday, we'd spend time together, our friendship was really close. So going to church to see Pamela was good enough for me.

But then they started separating us because we talked too much... Those days were hell, well maybe not hell, but definitely unbearable.

I didn't know how fond my memories of church were until years later. At the time, it felt like a punishment. It felt like you had to go to this place and stay for so long, and they preach, and they teach you about God but you don't really take it in. You go to different churches, meet different people, and you spend most of your life doing that until you're about 16 or 17 and you can't perm your hair, you can't pierce your ears, you can't wear trousers.

I remember feeling frustrated with this church thing in my early teens. I felt, *'Why do we have to do this? What is so sinful about lipsticks, and why would God personally have a problem with me wearing trousers? I know it's a male garment, but can't we just look at the jeans as a compromise?'*

I wanted to do what I wanted so badly that I was forced to wear my trousers under my skirt whenever I left my house. I'd roll them down when I got around the corner and apply the little bit of Constance Carroll make-up that I'd bought with my pocket money down the market. So I would leave my Christian home slightly sanctified and change into this little Godless child. When I got home, the trousers would be rolled back up and I'd use my sleeve to wipe away my Jezebel lipstick. Sanctified again.

As time went by, I started to rebel. "I can't do the church thing! Not another prayer meeting, no more conventions, stop taking me to Morris Cerullo and Selwyn Hughes and Billy Graham!" Kids today have the likes of T.D. Jakes but it wasn't so lively back then.

I was Jesus'd out. I wasn't a fan of all the church people, the little spies who were ready to tell my mum whenever they saw me talking to a boy on the street or comment on what I was wearing. '*It just won't do for a child coming from a Christian home, okay?*'

Regardless of the church people, I was going to live my life. Yes, I loved God, but if He's going to strike me down for straightening my hair, then so be it. I straightened my hair and the perm broke off most of my hair. Now was that a word from God? Who knows just how seriously God was taking the hairstyle...

I wanted to party too; I wanted some Carroll Thompson and Janet Kay. I wanted someone to ask me or even pull me onto the floor for a dance. I wanted to go to clubs and parties because life felt like a punishment without them. My friends would tell me about the wicked parties they were going to, the fantastic parties were they were meeting cute guys. They were even starting to date. I'd think, '*I have to go. I have to put on some lipstick and I want to wear a pair of trousers and party*' and I dreamed of being like them because the church wouldn't let me do it.

I remember sneaking out with my brothers once. We put pillows in our bed and we went to this party and I remember dancing and thinking, '*Oh, now I'm in heaven, now I'm in heaven. Surely this is what God wants, for me to be happy.*'

It was such a fantastic feeling, but only for a while. Arriving home, we tried our keys in the door, but it was locked. Trouble. My mum opened the door and threw a bucket of water at me and I thought, '*What do I do now?*' She shut the door on me and I had to go to my neighbour's and wait there until the next afternoon before she'd let me back in.

I didn't learn. Once I had the taste for the party life, there was no stopping me. I was going to sneak out better next time. I remember sneaking out and thinking, '*I'll do the church thing in the day, which means praise the Lord at church today, but I'm going to a party later and I can't wait.*'

When I started sneaking out to parties, it was time to start looking good and my church clothes didn't quite cut it. I remember this one party that was held at the time when there was that fashion for cowl-neck blouses. All the girls were wearing it; it had a loop through the centre of it that dipped at the chest. My mum was always a stylish lady and she had a blouse like that; it was such a lovely mustard colour and I remember thinking, *I'm going to wear my brown knitted skirt and that is the only blouse that will match and not only will it match, but it is the fashion blouse to wear and my mum's got it.*

I sneaked it out of her closet to wear that evening. When I padded up the bed this time, I bent the pillowcases to make the legs look more realistic. So I sneaked out and I'm looking so good, I'm wearing top fashion, my hair is curled, well, the best you could do with natural hair, flick over with soft curls. I'm hot, the boys are looking at me, and my friends think I look nice. Mrs Small, the lady who has these fantastic parties, greets me and asks if my mother knows I'm here. I lie and say she does, that she's happy for me to be here. Mrs Small looks at me, a bit worried.

I'm at this party and I'm having such a fantastic time, but guess where the party was? Next door.

The party was next door, given by a Bajan family and, by the way, they had the best parties. They would play their calypso…and they would have parties all the time so it wouldn't be strange for us to hear the party and not be there. I thought that it would be too obvious to go to the party and that would be precisely why my mum wouldn't think I'd dare. She'd think, *There is no way Angie would be stupid enough to go.*

So I'm at this party in my mum's blouse and I'm dancing, dancing, dancing and thinking this is fantastic, loving it. *Give it a couple of hours and I'll sneak back in.* The weather had turned cold, it was snowing outside, nothing to worry about, I only live next door. All of a sudden, the door opened and everybody's looking at me. I remember thinking, *Do I look that hot or what?'*

Then my friend mouthed to me, "Your mum's here." I remember thinking, *'Can you die from an overwhelming fear?'* I wanted to die, right now.

Then I'm taking this walk, this slow walk; it felt like the path had been lit for me already and everybody's looking at me. *"Oh my God, your mum's going to kill you!"* I heard a friend whisper; I wanted to look at her and say, *'I think you are right.'*

I remember walking to the door and my mum's standing there with her coat on over her nightie just waiting for me and then I remembered the blouse—her blouse. As I get to the door, she grabs it and it tears. She pulls at me. I'm slipping in the snow as she's dragging me and I'm like, *'Oh my God, she's tearing her clothes!'*

I was so scared. She dragged me inside and she looked at me and she looked at the blouse, and that infuriated her. I got a beating that night that never seemed to end. The next day, everyone was talking about what happened to me. "Angie got beaten on the street; Angie tore her mum's blouse." And you could hear the beating in the house because even though the party's going on next door, they're also listening for the beating.

Sometimes I feel that I could have had an easier life if church had been more lenient, if you could at least go to church and be able to say, "Look, I don't get what you're talking about right now, the intensity of it, I get it and I respect it, but I don't think it's for me right now."

Mum wasn't having that. I was always going to go. On a Wednesday night and a Friday night, she would have a prayer meeting so people would come over to the house and pray until about midnight or one in the morning. If your friends came around that evening, all they'd hear was, "Oh, yeah! Praise the Lord! Thank you, Jesus!" The sound of the prayer meeting would shake the house. Other neighbours would come around saying, "What's happening in your house?"

"Oh, my mum's friends are just laughing, they're just having fun." Yeah, right.

Then their meeting would finish and I'd have to go and make tea and biscuits and sit around and wait until they went to clean up. It was the routine, it was what it was, but after a while when I was getting older I started to think, *'I don't want to do this anymore,'* and I started to rebel.

I couldn't do it anymore and slowly my mum started to realise that maybe she couldn't force it now. When I was about 16 or 17, I'd oversleep and she'd leave me and I'd think, *'Okay, no problem, it's time to stop going to church.'*

The funniest thing is that that foundation was the making of me. You know, that discipline, that spirituality, that community, that understanding, that being able to go to that safe place. I always thought that everybody went to church, especially if you were black. I thought we all went to the same church and we all did the same thing. I soon found out that most of my friends didn't go to church and if they did, it was a Catholic church so they just said a few Hail Mary's and it was all good to go.

I thought, *'Wow, you've got a good church because you can wear make-up, you can straighten your hair.'*

I realised it was more of a Caribbean thing, this particular Pentecostal-type of church. I realised that religion could be very different with many beliefs and ways to worship God. I think it gave me strength throughout my life and I think I would've been a bit soulless if I hadn't spent my formative years in church. It grounded me completely.

Once I saw off church, I got straight into a more rebellious way of life. I realised I was pretty much free to go now and I could do more things, though there were still limits, of course. My parents were never going to let me do exactly what I wanted.

With my mum in Jamaica, still going to church.

Chapter 15:
You sure is ugly...

Clive had stood me up. We were supposed to meet at the Odeon to watch *The Color Purple*. I waited and waited but he didn't come, which didn't mean I was going home... I had done too much to get out of the house to see this movie with my boyfriend, and this was my idol, Whoopi Goldberg. I know I must have looked strange walking into the cinema by myself but I didn't care that people looked at me like I was some oddball without a boyfriend. *The Color Purple* was *my* movie and that classic line when Avery says to Celie, Whoopi Goldberg's character, "You sure is ugly..." always stuck with me.

It reminded me of growing up and trying to work out if I was pretty. You're not quite sure if you're pretty and you're not always sure if you are the marker, which is, are you the friend of the pretty one, or are you the pretty friend?

My brother told me once that he didn't want me to go to his secondary school because I was fat. And it's only looking back on it that I realise I wasn't fat and he didn't mean it, but I managed to make myself fat to make his words right. It's like you hear what people say about you, what they project on you, and sometimes you start to live it out. I guess it depends on your strength of character.

Looking at my friends, I'd think, *'Okay, she's pretty and she's pretty too, but I don't look like them, so I'm not pretty. When I'm with this friend, boys don't look at me, but if I'm with this friend, boys talk to me.'* When we were all together, I was the funny one in the group, and when I was by myself, the boys would ask about my pretty friend. I knew this friend was pretty because everyone looked at her and boys waited in line to chat her up while I was alone. *'I am not pretty, but I'm a nice girl who can make you laugh.'*

Then people would be like, *'If you were slimmer, you'd be beautiful because you have a good face.'* So I still don't have a pretty face, I have a Good Face, a face that is well-behaved, unlike my unruly hair. My hair is not good hair, it's not straight, another point lost right there.

Was I pretty? No. *'But you are not ugly,'* they said kindly. I was the funny friend and that was okay but the boys could have at least spared me a look while they were waiting in line for my friend.

So I tried working out where my prettiness stood on the pretty scale and thought, *'I'll go for good character, the reliable, funny friend who listens to all your boyfriend stories and tries to give you good advice.'* At the time, I didn't think of it as a character, I just thought, *'I'm gonna be funny, that will be my attractiveness. They will laugh so hard that they can't help but fancy me and fall in love with the funny girl, and then they'll see I'm beautiful.'*

Today I think that beauty comes with maturity and self-acceptance. Pretty is just what other people think of you. But when you are young, you can put yourself under extreme pressure. I didn't see many boys running after me in the playground. I didn't hear about my brothers' friends saying they fancied me and wanted to date me; that message wasn't coming back to me. I wasn't picking up on that, and believe me, I was keen to know.

I started to build on who I was, I started to enjoy myself and one day somebody looked at me... *'You're looking at me like you think I'm beautiful. Well the truth is, I am.'* I was in a club, feeling pretty, I think I was about

16; it was the time when I was still sneaking out and going to parties with my brothers. I felt safe with them. I knew everything was going to be okay. Those parties were quite dark; no one could see each other. When somebody found you attractive, they'd squeeze your elbow behind you to ask if they could have a dance.

There were no words, but you knew what to do. It was just a little squeeze on the elbow, and you turned around as though you were so grateful and then you started dancing. I remember that whole evening. I was dancing with different guys and I thought it was wonderful. Then I was in the groove but I was getting too close with this guy, just a little bit too close. All of a sudden, I felt someone touch my shoulders and pull me away.

My brother Rohan stood there and told the guy to go away because I was his sister. I remember thinking, *'Somebody kill me, just kill me right now. He wanted me, they wanted me and my brother stopped it.'* I couldn't believe how this was making me feel, and why was my brother still standing there? He was adamant that this whole affair was over. I looked at him, like, *'What's going on?'* He looked at me like, *'Not on my watch.'* I looked at him, like, *'Take your watch off then! I'm already not supposed to be here, it's all already wrong, why are we trying to make it right now?'*

Just go away, please, so he can dance with me… Okay, I'll just dance by myself and listen to this rocking lovers rock music, and be here by myself with all these guys pulling me to dance, and I'll just point at my brother, because he's to blame, and then I'll keep my head straight.

Chapter 16:
Teenage love

My mum and dad used to wonder what they were going to do with me. It was clear my head was only focused on one thing. I was into the Arts; give me a stage, give me an audience, and I was at peace. So I was at the drama clubs, the workshops, drama schools, trying to get myself in that performance world because I knew from a young child that is what I wanted to do, so my teenage years were really about finding myself in that world.

I loved the arts, but when I went to college I started noticing all these nice-looking boys… They were bringing up some feelings in me, feelings that I had not planned for. *'Why am I looking at this boy with these feelings? Why am I dreaming about him when I go home? Why am I writing stories about running through the sand in the moonlight? Oh. My. God. I fancy Clive!'*

I thought Clive was far too good-looking for me. Everybody in college fancied him, and I fancied him, but I didn't think that he would like me, it was too ambitious. Pitch yourself at a reasonable place, Angela; everybody liked him. I mean, the pretty girls liked him, and they stood a much better chance. I kept telling myself to focus on my drama classes and get on with the dream and let go. He was one of the guys who would be in the common room playing bar football, they were always on it, and nobody could beat them and get them off it. They were brilliant. So I thought, *'Well I'm going to learn to how to play bar football so that I can get his attention and beat him and I will be this girl that he couldn't beat.'* A bit ambitious, I know, well actually impossible.

I remember playing bar football and being dressed up. I'd bought a new outfit, a blue jacket in What She Wants in Peckham. I was looking quite hot, my hair was in two twists, with a little extension, just to add a little perk, and I had a bit of make-up on, red lipstick. *I'm going to look really good, the best I can and just play bar football and act like he's not there.'* It was a mad plan, but I really liked him.

I remember sitting there thinking, *'He is so good looking...'*

I was looking hot, well I thought so. I remember him looking at me, and I'm looking at him thinking, *'Does he fancy me too? He must, he's looking at me rather intense. I haven't started playing yet. Can I just get on with my plan so I can beat him at this game?'*

Here we go, ten pence on the table corner. Bridget was playing. Now no one can beat her, she's pretty, a very cool chick, she has it all, and she's champion at bar football. I'm taking my ten pence and going home! I'm up next. Clive beckons me over, no jokes to save me, just serious concentration.

I didn't beat him, but I did very well, and that was it.

We started talking. After that, I knew he fancied me so I didn't need to learn the game. Clive became my first boyfriend. Lots of sneaking around, lots of phone calls planned because if he phoned my home and my dad picked the phone up, and there was a boy there, then there were going to be a lot of problems, so I was like, "You have to call me at seven o'clock."

I had a boyfriend: I am woman! It was a fun relationship, lots of creeping around, none of that taking him home to meet my family. Are you crazy?! No, we don't do that at my house! At home I would just hang around the phone, and if my parents caught me talking to a boy, I would have to put the handset down immediately. We spent a lot of time at his home, and his mother was lovely. It was one of those college romances; we weren't too open about the relationship there, which was okay. Being in a relationship at that stage of my life was quite exciting because I couldn't tell many people, so it didn't really get the audience it could have got. He really made me laugh and that was all that mattered at that point in my life.

This relationship went on for about two years. Although you couldn't call it serious, I thought I loved him. I was going to marry him, and we were going to have children, they were going to be twins, and they were going to be called Clive and Clivinia. I thought that was going to be it and then I found out he was seeing somebody else from college… *'Oh. So that's why we are keeping this romance quiet, it isn't to protect me, it's to protect you.'*

I couldn't sleep at nights, my first heartbreak; I was devastated. Okay, that's a bit dramatic and I have to admit that a part of me liked what I was experiencing. I'd read about it in all those magazines, *My Guy* and *Jackie*. I was hurting. I looked at my tear-stained face in the mirror and felt a kind of satisfaction; now I too could write into the agony sections. But as you get older, you realise it's nothing new, you and the whole world go through it.

Then Clive would swear that I was the only one…you know, like they do… and I believed him until I found out again that I wasn't the only one! But he was such a likeable person; it was so easy to forgive him. It took a while for me to move on from my college romance and get on with life.

Chapter 17:
Bemarro Sisters doing it for themselves

How lucky was I to have my closest friends living only a road away from me? This friendship was formed at Lewisham Youth Drama Group, which was run by Dave Green at that time. We lived for Wednesday and Friday evenings.

If we weren't at the drama group, we were dressing up and going to raves or the theatre. Wednesday night was our weekly visit to Gullivers Nightclub. We would dress up and catch the 36 bus to the West End. Then we'd get the night bus home. If we ordered a taxi, our local cab driver Jesse would pick us up. He always said, "Even if you have no money, call me. You girls are like daughters to me." Awesome man!

We were active young women. After watching many theatre productions over the years, we wanted to create our own work so the four of us formed a theatre group. There was me and three other young girls, Marie Berry and the sisters, Debbie and Beverley Rose. We used our surnames to come up with our group's name, 'The Bemarro Sisters'—Berry, Martin, and Rose.

We had our theatre company and we realised quite early that we were going to have to write and produce our own plays. We created one called *The Slice Of Life* with Pauline Jacobs who wrote it for us, Debbie Rose and Collette Johnson. It was about young black women in different scenarios.

Our lives were filled with excitement; we went everywhere together. We loved music. Debbie was the oldest. She was very mature, she had boyfriends and wouldn't always be with us; she was always busy, studying—she seemed to have a fun life without us. She had a serious collection of music—Phyllis Hyman, The Jones Girls, Tina Turner, all the 80s hits—and our afternoons were filled with music pouring out of the PA system in her bedroom. We'd pretend to be all the stars with hairbrushes as the mic. There wasn't a day we weren't dressed up and made up, even if it was just to play our favourites stars. We'd mime to the songs over and over again, but Beverley didn't have to because she could really sing.

We'd spend the afternoons working out what we were going to wear and how we were going to show off our latest fashion and up-to-date hairstyles. Beverley and Debbie had their own unique style; there was never a chance of going out and seeing anyone else in their clothes. Marie was unique in her way too; we would often call her Mad Mar because she would put some mad creations together and pull off an amazing look. I think I was the boring, safe dresser; I think that was the church girl in me. We honestly enjoyed each other, but the greatest thing about it was that we lived so close to each other—it was the making of us. We always said we'd stick together through thick and thin; we were tight and extremely protective of each other. Boyfriends struggled with our friendship because if you upset one of us, you had three to deal with. Sometimes we crossed the line and I believe that this was one of the issues that started to wear us down. There were a few occasions when boyfriends were confronted by the sisters; once we'd heard enough, we were off.

A creative group of young women, we were relentless in what we thought we could do. Writing and producing plays became normal for us. We raised money for productions. We were strong together. We took our work to everywhere, across England, Holland. We lived in the theatre once we left Lewisham Youth Drama. We wanted more, so we started at the Albany

Empire. We joined Second Wave with the outrageous Cathy Kilcoyne. We learned about productions, we wrote, we directed, we produced. *A Net Full of Holes* was our first production with Second Wave.

It was an adventure; we'd even spent some time at the daily afternoon sessions at Barbara Speake Stage School. It took us nearly two hours to get there every day, but we didn't care, we felt we were studying the Arts.

When we walked into a drama class in Brixton's Dick Sheppard School, we knew we had found the right place for us. Afro Sax, run by actors Larrington Walker, Ellen Thomas and Treva Etienne, was awesome: we had finally found our home. They got us, they encouraged us, and we loved and trusted everything they shared with us.

Afro Sax and the Albany were the making of me. The teachers didn't play around; Larrington was like the strict headmaster, you didn't mess around with him. He was stern in his teaching, he wanted us to take this seriously and we did; he called us his beautiful bouquet. Ellen was like the stunning big sister; to this day, she shares the dos and don'ts of the business—how to present yourself, what not to expect, how to deal with difficult situations. It was a special relationship. She was our first mentor. It was important to have a black woman guiding us, truly explaining what this business was about. Watching her at work was like having our very own drama school. Treva had a special gift; he was always so encouraging; he believed you could do anything. There were times you left so pumped up, you'd take the improvisations onto the streets. We never wanted to go home after class. As the youngest teacher, he was able to play on both sides of his role; he would get so much out of you and he truly believed in change. That place was filled with energy; the talent that came from Afro Sax was extraordinary.

The Bemarro Sisters was a force to be reckoned with for about seven years. I think towards the end of our relationship, we just outgrew each other. It was something we never expected. Unfortunately, the ending was painful for all;

the friendship was starting to crack, it started to turn sour, we were getting angry and frustrated with each other. We'd been told that we'd outgrow each other, but we rejected it. We knew we were going to be together through thick and thin.

We loved what we did; this was who we were. We were going to write and travel all over England with our plays; this was the perfect friendship. We had already achieved so much. We were in each other's skin; it's what friendship was supposed to be. We were perfect together, dependant on each other. We would do anything for each other, and I mean anything. We lived through each other's experience. We learned about relationships through Debbie; she would tell us about her boyfriends, we would watch her get dressed and disappear into the night. There were nights we would make up our own stories and talk about the boys we liked, the fashion shows we had gone to and how much we fancied the models Delroy Dyer, Barrie Thomas and Anthony Howard. We would act out the fashion show, pretending to be the guys, imagining how they looked at us, and we'd laugh at our own stupidity. Delroy lived around the corner from us so we often went to the shops dressed up to the nines.

But change came when the boyfriends appeared on the scene. I remember when I met David. I met him very early. The girls didn't take to him at first, I suppose because they were worried that he would split up the group. I had convinced them that I didn't fancy him, we were just friends. But he was my distraction and it was as though the other Bemarro Sisters thought this guy was taking me away from them, which he wasn't, not as far as I was concerned anyway. He was always around after the shows. It started to get awkward for me as I tried to keep both sides sweet. It was a horrible time. It would start by me not being available to go out with them as often as we used to. I was always disappearing after our shows, trying to split my time between my friends and my boyfriend.

My response was becoming irritating… "I can't make it; I'm going somewhere else already." That was always hard to say and it was so difficult to separate because if there was a problem in the relationship, you'd tell your friends, and when it was sorted out and you were happily back with your boyfriend, your friends might not find it so easy to let it go.

It started to cause real tension between us. We were pretty much on our last legs. I went to Jamaica and when I came back, there was a resignation letter from them. We had formed a company and we could resign from it at any time, but receiving that letter alongside a pile of clothes on the bed was hard. We used to wear each other's clothes, and now here were all my trousers, jackets, jumpers, everything. *'Oh my God, this is it, my friends have gone.'*

I cried. I cried because of our dreams, our aspirations. We still had plays to write, still had the world to conquer. But now it was over, and that hurt has never really left me.

The Bemarro Sisters. Beverley Rose, myself and Marie Berry.

The team behind Afro Sax where we, the Bemarro Sisters, found our home. Actors Ellen Thomas, Larrington Walker (above) and Treva Etienne (below).

Chapter 18:
My Dave

How do you meet the man of your dreams? You start dating his best friend and then get to know him from a distance. It was never my intention, but I believe it was fate.

I found dating really awkward, in fact my husband David told me he found me quite awkward. I don't feel I was like a normal girlfriend, I wasn't really experienced, I didn't have the young dating experience, I wasn't allowed out, so I was new to a lot of this.

When I started dating this particular young man called Glenn, I was truly smitten. He was good-looking, very tall, in fact too tall; I was always in heels, even at the beach, trying not to look like his daughter.

It was an odd relationship in the early days. I thought we got on well, although he was a little different in his style and presentation, quite straight really. When I think back now, he must have thought I was a silly young girl. I was far too trusting; I used to believe everything he said. If he said he was at his mum's, well, that's where he should be, surely. I think he saw me coming; there were so many incidents where I should have picked up that things were not quite as he was telling me.

We would plan to go out. I'd spend hours getting ready and then I would sit there waiting patiently. My family would keep asking me, "Aren't you going out? Why are you dressed up and sitting in the house?" Yep, I'd been stood up in my own house yet again! Each time Glenn was either extremely late or he wouldn't turn up at all, which made me worry about him. I had no way of contacting him, so I'd worry from Friday night until Monday morning. I'd think maybe he had died and there was no way for me to find out until I phoned his workplace on Monday—after calling his best friend David every few hours to see if he had seen his friend, or if he had in fact died. I would call his flat where he lived with his sister. This woman scared the life out of me; she was so miserable; she'd scream down the phone, and tell me not to call back. I wondered if she was upset because maybe he had died and she wasn't dealing with it. No, she was just miserable.

Every Monday, he'd pick up the phone cool as a cucumber with no idea that he had been on the missing persons list. He would make some silly excuse, usually something to do with his mother, sickness, or car trouble. I couldn't prove it, so we continued with the farce.

I was finally invited to meet his people at his cousin's wedding. He told me he was going to take me there and I would meet his family, his mum and the sister from the end of the phone. *'Oh, dear,'* I thought. *'Well at least it means I'm serious, I am his woman.'*

My mum made my outfit; I went to Panache in Dalston and picked out some shoes to go with my red dress.

We walked into the wedding together, and that was it, he disappeared, gone for hours. I sat at the reception smiling with strangers, strangers who questioned who I was with; they seemed shocked by our status. I went to the toilet to freshen up, and there it was, the confrontation that we'd all been waiting for, the girlfriend, *the real girlfriend*, who wanted to tell me my boyfriend had done a runner. I was accused of all sorts of things. There

I was, waiting on this man, and he'd left me to face his girlfriend and her cousin alone.

His friend David took me home. He felt so sorry for this little South London girl all the way out there in East London, a fish out of water who had no way to get home. I couldn't understand why my boyfriend had done it; what a waste of time!

Glenn was at my house first thing in the morning explaining that this girl was mad, she wouldn't accept that it was over, and all I could think was, *'Well I hope you are not like her and that you can accept that this is over.'*

The funny thing is David and I had become such good friends. The first time I met him, I didn't like him, I thought he was arrogant. He drove a blue Ford Capri, and how he loved his car! He did look great in it, especially when he was smoking, the smoke whirling slowly out of the window as we coughed. He looked like he was in the movies with his eyes squinting slightly as he blew the coolest smoke rings in all kinds of sizes. I wanted to scream, "How do you do that?" but how could I—an upstanding young girl raised in the church—be impressed by a young man smoking?

The first time I met him, it was snowing and he had come to pick me up with my boyfriend. We were going to play badminton. My house was on a hill and David refused to drive up the road because it was icy. I had to walk down the slippery pavement holding onto Glenn, and all the time I was thinking, *'What a cheek, how dare he make me walk down in the snow! It's unacceptable, who does this? Why are we accepting this behaviour?'*

I questioned my boyfriend every step of the way, complaining about the disrespectful treatment I was suffering. Just what type of man was this?

I sat in the cool car, thinking, *'How dare he do this to me.'* I was dressed in my new pink tracksuit ready to play badminton, well I knew we were going to play badminton, but I had never played before. I was being cute, hence the lovely pink tracksuit, but I didn't intend to sweat. I wasn't going to be athletic, that wasn't my thing except for football or netball, none of which were needed right now.

We started playing and it's over as soon as it starts. *'If this guy is going to keep sending me to the other side of the court, then it's not going to work. Why is he working this game so hard? Why is my boyfriend allowing this to happen?'*

They asked if I had played before. How rude! *'That's not the point, please respect the pink tracksuit.'* I decided to sit the rest of the game out, I had done enough running up and down and I didn't need to put myself through any more, especially when I felt someone was trying to teach me a lesson. Needless to say, we drove home through the snow in silence. I was looking out the window, thinking, *'This Ford Capri does not impress me in the slightest. I much prefer my boyfriend's Datsun Cherry, at least it moves sometimes, just not today.'*

I didn't think I fancied David, not at all. We would talk, we would talk a lot. I would call him all the time to see if he knew where my so-called boyfriend was, and yes, of course, he would cover up for him. When all the mess at the wedding happened, which was similar to what had happened at another party a few months before, I forgave him. There were so many signs, I mean, you'd have to be really missing something to not get that this boyfriend of mine was a player. He must have wondered to himself, *'Why doesn't this girl get it? How many situations can you get yourself into, ex-girlfriends confessing that your boyfriend is a joker, and not to take him seriously?'*

David said to me, after many calls and sad conversations with me feeling really hurt, "Angie, you are a nice girl and I don't want to keep lying to you. He isn't the one for you, you have to let go of him. He's not serious. I'm really sorry; he has always been engaged to that girl."

I wasn't too broken up about it and I appreciated his honesty. Then it hit me that I'd have no more excuses to call David! But I couldn't stop calling

David, he was just so nice. I wasn't even thinking about a relationship, he was already in one anyway, so to me he was off-limits. I'd call him to tell him about auditions and then call him back to say why I hadn't got the part. He'd wish me luck and say, "You'll get the next one." Luther was David's all-time favourite singer, so obviously I'd have to call him to find out if he'd heard Luther's latest album, and, of course he had so then we had to talk about each track and analyse all the lyrics. Maybe I was going too far, but at least we kept in touch.

Then one day, he asked me to go and see Patti Labelle with him. I was truly excited, he knew I loved Patti! I was so excited; I could picture her walking onto the stage, reaching those high notes. I wore a purple shirt donated by my Bemarro Sister Marie. We did what we always did, we rehearsed my outfit and had a mini-fashion show: sit, stand, cough, laugh with my hands on my chest, flick the hair, walk forward, walk back, do it again until it is perfect!

I waited in leather trousers and purple suede high heels, but I didn't fancy him, I was just going out with a friend. I graduated my hair; the layers were looking great, but where was he? He was late; we missed Patti, that's right, once in a lifetime Patti. I couldn't believe I wasn't angry, but it was okay, I was with him, although I never fancied him. So we walked the King's Road, stopped in at Blushes and had a few drinks, and drove around in his car with the windows down, listening to Patti. We laughed, we talked, and he was such a nice person. *'If I had a boyfriend, I'd like him to be like David,'* but, of course, I didn't fancy him.

David never mentioned to me that he had broken up with his girlfriend. Our friendship got stronger; I needed to share everything with him. Then I realised something had changed. We spoke every day; he would drive down and we would go and get something it eat, and talk all night in the car. This went on for weeks and then one day, as I stood at my doorway, saying goodbye, trying to be quiet, trying not to wake my parents, clearly the conversation was over, and I thought, *'So how come he's still standing there?'*

It happened. He reached over and gave me that kiss, the one that said I fancy you and I can't hold it back any longer. The next day he called to see how I really felt about it. I was like, *'I'm okay...'* and acted all lost and confused, but in my head I was thinking, *'You'd better do that again!'*

It was official, David was my boyfriend. Now I had to explain to my friends that it seemed I did fancy him after all. I had to try to explain to my family, yes, that was my boyfriend's friend, yes, it's him. I know, amazing, right!

Chapter 19:
Pregnant…oops…

I don't know why I thought having sex with my boyfriend would keep me immune from becoming pregnant, I mean, really! Anyway, it wasn't in my plan. I came from a strict background, and pregnancy wasn't on my to-do list. It was one of my mum's instructions, 'DO NOT GET PREGNANT!' Okay, I get that, like I have sex anyway! Oh, ye of little faith.

And I got pregnant. I remember thinking when I was five months' gone, *'How did that happen? I'm on the pill…ish.'* I found out very late. It just wasn't registering that I was pregnant because I still had mild periods.

It was a difficult time. My friendship with my Bemarro Sisters was on and off, we still had work commitments and when we needed each other, we would still show up. And how I needed them now! I was distraught, pregnancy was not in the plan. *'I have things to do, my mum will kill me, I've let her down, this isn't what she wanted for me, what will the church say, how will I look? I can't have this child! Please make it stop, make it go away.'* I was so scared. Was I going to let the Bemarro Sisters down too? We had things to do and shows booked. Even though we were finished as a company, the strained friendship was still there, trying to fix itself.

I went to a consultation at an abortion clinic. I don't know what I was thinking; I didn't even know that this was an option... I couldn't cope with it. The doctor said, "You can't have a straight abortion at this stage, at five months. If you do, you have to have a cold labour. You'd stay awake and you would just give birth to the dead foetus at five months." *What?*

I was very scared of telling my parents. This would be the worst thing because my mum was always fearful of me being an actress; you know that 'don't put your daughter on the stage' idea. But now I had to tell her. That was a sad day for us. The Bemarro Sisters were feeling it for me. I was so lost; I remember squeezing into my trousers, being in complete denial. Everything was flashing forward, I couldn't live my dream anymore, and I couldn't do all things we'd planned as a group. *'I'm pregnant!'*

I knew I couldn't have an abortion because I wouldn't be able to live with myself. I was at five months; there were only four months to go. Could it be that bad? Would my mother throw me out, would my dad be disappointed with his only daughter? As we walked home, I knew my friends could feel the weight of my decision, a decision that I had to make alone, even though they kept reminding me, *'We're sisters through thick and thin.'* David was just as shocked, but wanted to get on with it and make it work.

I remember that walk home, saying goodbye to my friend Beverley, and getting closer to home and saying goodbye to my last friend Marie. She stopped me and said, "You can't do it, can you?"

"No, I can't. It's not me."

I got home and walked straight into my mum's room and told her I was pregnant. She was shocked, but it wasn't until days later that she reacted. She was very upset, "Oh God, oh God, oh God, oh God, oh why, why?" One of those.

My dad was like, "What? When? How did that happen?" Throughout his shocked reaction and Mum's odd outburst about me having sex and getting pregnant, I just kept still and quiet. She needed to let off her frustrations, and then she would calm down and make sure I was eating, and drinking carrot juice and beetroot juice. She would shop at Mothercare, buying everything. My dad prepared my room, new wallpaper, new lamps, and new radiators.

It was always going to be difficult telling my brothers, because to them their little sister didn't have sex. My brothers were angry with me and my boyfriend. Everyone went into overdrive. "What are we going to do with this pregnant girl?" Decisions were being made around me, the family was kicking in. My boyfriend and I were going through it, the pressure was on. We hadn't planned this, but we just had to get on with it: it was a horrible time.

Once your baby is born, the world carries on as though it's no big deal. But I changed. I was a mother; I had to do things differently. My mum was adamant that she would support me, and I was to carry on with my dreams. I performed right through the pregnancy and two weeks after giving birth, I was back on stage. Nothing was going to stop me, especially now.

We got over the shock and got on with it. Mum would have her moments, "I can't believe you got yourself pregnant. Why, why, why?" And then she'd get back to the shopping.

This was their second grandchild. Their first one Nicolas was from Rohan. As I was their only daughter, I was very close to them and when that baby was born, it was as though they were in heaven. Some of the church members were upset with Mum because they thought she should have thrown me out. My mum just said, "Not my daughter, not my daughter. There's no way."

I think she took a lot of stick from the church for that because she stood her ground. My mum and dad were perfect for me because I could get on with my shows and my mum said, "Nothing is going to change. You are going to continue; you're going to do what you have to do and we're all here for you." My dad would pick up my son from school. My parents were second to none. "We'll just get on with it; you know we all make mistakes. You've made a mistake and it's there, and we're going to deal with it." That's when I really learned what unconditional love is.

Chapter 20:
Dreams

I remember when my brother Michael first said, "What the mind can conceive, the man can achieve." It never left me; I remember thinking that I could do anything and I was always encouraged by my parents to fly. My mum would say, "You can do whatever you want to do in life." If things didn't go to plan, she'd say "Take every setback as a springboard to go forward."

She had so many good quotes that told me it was alright to dream and believe that I could do anything and be somebody, I really could do something quite amazing. When I was at school, as much as I felt stupid or left behind or less intelligent than the rest, I still knew I was clever, as odd as that sounds. I still felt special. I felt like there was something about me that had got something to do, and I just didn't know what it was going to be yet. I remember watching Whoopi Goldberg and Richard Pryor and Joan Rivers; it reminded me how I used to be as a child always cracking jokes. I loved the sound of laughter. When I heard laughter, it told me that I was in the right zone. I'm in my zone, and when I make people laugh, I know that is my blessing from God. But how was I going to take this blessing and turn it into something? And that's when I started to dream about becoming a star. But it wasn't just about having fame and fortune, that wasn't the thing that did it for me; stardom wasn't expected for me but I wanted to be recognised for what I could do. That's when I started to think about becoming a stand-up comic.

I remember one of my first stand-up gigs. It was at a dance and I remember thinking, *'If I can make black people laugh…you know, I think I can do it if I just get them to like me.'*

You know when you go to a club and they're partying, it's dark, the music is playing, it's called a blues dance? That was where I had my first gig. I felt brave enough to ask the DJ if I could have the mic to tell a few jokes. I look back on that night and think I was mad and brave. I remember the DJ introducing me saying, with a thick West Indian Jamaican accent, "We have a gal who wants to tell two jokes, I beg unno move back."

I thought, "*Wow, what an introduction.*"

Now I really had to be funny because they were dancing together really close, they were sweating, concentrating, the music was sweet. Something this delicate is called scrubbing and in this intimate zone, relationships are formed, children could be made tonight, and they looked happy enough without me interrupting them to tell some jokes. I knew it could be touch and go, but it was too late…

"Ladies, do you know what it's like when you're walking down the street and a guy shouts, 'psst'? And you want to go, 'Excuse me, who are you talking to? My name is not psst, it's Carol. What do you want anyway?'"

I made all these jokes about relationships, friends, wearing a weave and how you scratch one side and the other side moves. All these women were looking back at me, laughing, they could relate. I was winning at this blues dance, the sisters and brothers were giving me the thumbs up. *'That's my story,'* they thought. As my confidence grew, I started to talk about growing up with West Indian parents. For the first time, black women saw a black woman joking about who we were! *'I am you, and I've got the same stories. I look like you, I can make your story funny too, we exist as well and it's going to be alright.'*

I became Britain's first black female stand-up comedienne, and I didn't realise at the time what that meant, I was just busy doing my thing out there in the clubs, the blues, the conferences, Venues, Podium, Penthouse, even AGM meetings, the fashion shows from Tony Wellington's Finesse Modelling Agency and the award dinners—I was everywhere a group of black people were gathered.

After many years of this, the comedy circuit opened up, and then the black comedy circuit. I was so in demand, I worked most nights. The fact is if you wanted to book a black person and a woman, you'd book me, I was two for one.

I was in three or four gigs a night sometimes, I was that busy on the circuit. It dawned on me that I was a real comic; I was a stand-up comedienne telling jokes. I walked into places and I was doing the same thing there that I'd been doing in my dining room as a child whenever there was a blackout. Now I was being paid to do this and the more I did it, the better I got, and the audience loved me.

Performing at a nightclub Penthouse Suite, age 18.

Performing, age 19 years old, at Club Podium in Vauxhall, London.

John Simmits Upfront Comedy, with Aymer and Powell, John, and Felix Dexter. Mid 80s

Over 30 years of stand-up, and still standing.

Chapter 21:
Funny Black Women on the Edge

Television was coming in and radio was coming in, and I thought, *'I can do this, but now I've got to do it on a bigger scale.'* Business was getting better; the requests were coming fast… "Can Angie do this? Can Angie do that?" Sure, sure, sure. "We would love to see Angie for this role; we hear she's an actress too."

I'd always known the words would catch up with me one day; this reading aloud thing was coming back to haunt me, I knew it. I started going to a few auditions; I didn't get them all because the dyslexic part of me came into the audition too. When I'm on stage, it's all good because they are all my words, but when I go to auditions, they are somebody else's words.

That's when I started to think, *'Wait a minute, I can't do this, it doesn't work.'* They would look at me like I'm the big Angie Le Mar. I started to feel under serious pressure because I knew I couldn't do stand-up forever, but I didn't think I could cross over into the acting world, so what would I do instead?

I used to watch *French and Saunders* on television and see these white women cracking jokes and doing sketches. I started thinking, *'Where are the black women? Why aren't the black women there too? Why can't we do more than this?'*

I didn't see myself as a writer but my brother Michael had said to me, "What the mind can conceive, the man can achieve." So I went to Canada and I wrote this show because I had just found a group of actors, we had just finished doing panto together, *Cinderella*, a huge success. I met some great comedic actresses and we were all getting on so well and I thought, *'I'm going to write a show for us.'*

So I went and wrote *Funny Black Women on the Edge*. I wanted to make it clear: we are funny, we are black, we are women, and we are on the edge. We're going to write sketches, we're going to be sexy, we're going to be edgy, we're going to be funky, we're going to be all the things that white comediennes are allowed to be, and we were going to do it in that show. I went to the Civic Centre in Peckham and met with Ian Thomson, the Managing Director at the time; he was so encouraging, he understood what we had and he booked the show.

It was so exciting for me. I loved writing it; it showed us our versatility as actors, but above all we were able to be hilarious. We didn't have the budget for directors, costumes, or set designers, so I directed it myself with the help of my close friend, Shade Oladiti. We went to the markets for our costumes. We made the set, borrowing stuff from my mum who also helped make the costumes. We bought wigs, we begged, we borrowed. No, we didn't steal!

I didn't know what to expect. All I knew was that when I was writing it, it made me laugh and that's all I had to go with. Now it was time for the audience to decide, and they loved it. We opened the show as En Vogue. The audience understood from the beginning where we were taking it; that we had something to say too. The cast was fantastic; we knew we had something special which would run for years.

The audience came out in big numbers. All I kept seeing when I drove up to the theatre were the same two words: Sold Out. I kept thinking, *'But don't they know I'm not a writer?'* Luckily I didn't have to audition, or I would have never got a part. I just wrote something I believed in and the success was so unexpected, the rave reviews and the love. Then my agent at the time, Debi Allen, said, "I'm taking the show to the Edinburgh Festival."

I thought, *'Wow!'* I made up a flyer that made us look like we could be singers because I wanted to go against the expected image. My agent said, "Don't expect any more than 15 people each night. There are about two thousand shows in Edinburgh so be very careful." She said we should expect about four or five people a night.

We sold out from the opening night right to the end. We sold out! My agent came into the dressing room and said, "Is anybody using these chairs?"

"Why?"

"Because you've sold out opening night!"

We didn't hide. Sometimes people would say, "Why are you calling it black? Why can't you just say *Funny Women on the Edge*? Why don't you put a white woman in there?" And I kept thinking, *'Because you've got those shows already. This is for us. If I did that, I'd write myself out of this and right now, no one's writing us in so it's 'Funny Black Women on the Edge.''*

When we came back, we went to the theatre and saw, Sold Out, Sold Out, Sold Out. I thought, *'I've taken control here, I've got the power of the pen.'* I remember working with a director years ago, Decima Francis, and she said to me, "The power is in the pen. When you can write your story, you're a winner." I thought, *'Does that mean I might write another show?'* I started to realise, *'Wait a minute, this thing works!'*

After *Funny Black Women on the Edge*, I got such great publicity that I got picked to do some stand-up on *The Real McCoy*.

Chapter 22:
"You're listening to Angie Le Mar on..."

I was moving into different areas, but one area I never really considered professionally was radio. I had done a few pirate stations in the past, like LWR, but that was a while ago and it was time to get back in the studio.

I starred in Channel 4's hit series *Get Up Stand Up* as a radio DJ who did a late night call-in show. The character gave terrible advice, but she was a cool, soulful chick with a sultry voice. Who knew that a comedy sketch show would land me a radio show just like the show I was spoofing?

I was invited into Greater London Radio (GLR), or Radio London as we all know it now. Gloria Abramoff wanted to meet and offer me a late night radio show. I tried to explain that I wasn't a radio host, but she was convinced I had what it took. "Just come in and meet me," she said. "You already have the voice, I heard it in the sketch, and you're a comedienne, it's a no-brainer! Just be yourself, you will come across like a natural."

That's all I needed and I went for it. I took over from Bob Mills and had a hit radio show. My producer, Ray Paul, was so patient with me, he understood the dyslexia and my fears, and made me sound like a real radio host, until even I started to believe it.

I enjoyed myself there and when I left, I went to Choice FM. I was at the station one afternoon putting on some adverts for a show I was producing when I saw the Managing Director, Patrick Berry. I said to him, semi-joking, "I'd love to have a show. Have you got a show for me? When can I start?"

He said, "Okay. What sort of a show would it be?"

This is what you call thinking quick on your feet; I guess being a comic, you are always thinking quickly. I went into overdrive because I had to appear as though I was always thinking about doing this show, like it was a real passion. I totally went for it!

I said it would be called *Ladies' Room* because that's the room where ladies talk, but men like to listen in too. It would only be on once a week for an hour. There'd be a phone-in, special guests, and lively debates.

"Okay, let's get you trained."

Trained! I didn't want to drive the desk; I just wanted to do the talking. "Not at Choice, love," said Ivor Etienne, the Programme Controller. I tried to explain: "I don't drive the desk. I used to have my producer. I do it differently. You see, at the BBC, I had Ray Paul. Ray did all of this for me…" *'You're not listening,'* I thought.

My training started straightaway. It took nearly a year of patient teaching before my brain understood the board. I may have been a bit stubborn too… I wanted Ivor to give up and just let me have a producer, but he didn't give up. And to this day, I am still so proud to walk into any radio station and be able to say, "Yes, I drive the desk too…duh!" Radio became so special to me; I slowly understood the power of the airwaves.

I was at Choice for nearly ten years. Before I knew it, I went from the late night show to the Saturday morning show, taking over from a well-loved DJ. It was a controversial takeover, one that I thought about very carefully before stepping into his place, especially as he was a friend. I contacted him to discuss the offering and he gave me his blessing. So *the Angie Le Mar Saturday Morning Show* was born. It was one of the highest-rated shows on the weekend for a long time.

Chapter 23:
Blag it, but back it!

Don't pray for opportunities; just be ready when they come. There were times when I would think, *'Just let me have a go, I will prove myself. If you show me once, I'll get it, just give me an opportunity.'* I would give anything a go, within reason. I don't worry too much about looking good, or being cool; I just trust that whatever happens, I'll be able to handle it. This business is full of blaggers, people who just want to be given a chance to do something.

I was asked to make a show for the BBC's *Video Diaries*. They gave you a camera operator and time to go away and create a documentary about your life. I was going to America to try out the comedy circuit and just see how I would do over there. I was going for 11 weeks, hitting the clubs, the radio shows; being black and British was pretty much opening doors for me. And now I'm in America, playing at the Harlem Apollo.

How did I get that gig? I walked up to the office and said, "I'd like to meet Chuck Sutton." I had done my research on who was running the Apollo and he was the Managing Director. He came downstairs with security because I'm sure they thought I was mad.

"So how can I help you, Mrs Le Mar?"

"Well, I'd like to play the Apollo. It's always been my dream to play the Apollo."

He said, "You're going to be my special guest tomorrow night."

I said, "Thank you very much. Fine, I'll see you tomorrow," and inside I was going, "*YES!*" I was in complete shock, I had all the reasons why I should be playing at the Apollo, I had my script just in case he said, "Go away, you mad lady!" I'd been prepared to fall down and scream and cry. But he just said yes…

So I'm going to the Apollo now, they've got a 300-seat theatre, and they've got a 700-seat theatre, and I play in the 3,000-seater. I get on the stage and they give me this big introduction, "All the way from London, England, we have the one, the only, give it up for Angie Le Mar!" And I was thinking, *'It's too much, pull it back in, you're making me sound good.'*

I was so nervous. After walking up the stairs and looking at the pictures, the Hall of Fame, all the legends that had played here at the Harlem Theatre, here I was, a little black girl from Lewisham walking onto the stage, being greeted with a big round of applause.

I went out there and it started well, they loved the British accent. I didn't want to overstay my welcome as I thought maybe I was losing them. Then it got a bit ropey, so I just said, "Goodnight, thank you and goodbye." The feeling was awesome, but I was still so nervous. Chuck said, "They love you, Angie, come back anytime."

All of this was being filmed for BBC's *Video Diaries*. I'm being filmed in New York doing all this stuff! Then I thought, *'I want to audition for The Cosby Show.'* I called them up and said in my best British accent, "Angie Le Mar is here from London, but she's only doing a few interviews. Would you like to see her?"

They're like, "If she's here, then we must see her." Thank God they didn't have Google! So I met them and they let me read Phylicia Rashad's bit from *The Cosby Show* because, guess what, they're casting a new sitcom called *A Different World* and they think I would be very good as a British teacher and I'm thinking, *'This sounds fantastic but I have to go to LA...'* I contact the BBC to share this wonderful news, and they tell me, "No, you can't stay in New York, you're contracted to go to LA for this documentary. So the BBC decided that I couldn't do it and I had to go. I know; it's a different world.

Chapter 24:
Stand in your hustle

I trust that I can get into most rooms and I have been in many situations where I have really had to trust my hustle. Like there was this time when I just had to go and see Joan Rivers at the Queen's Theatre in London. I was so in awe of Joan, I had to get my poster signed! I went backstage and saw the big crowd waiting for autographs. I could tell that most were waiting in vain, she may sign two or three with just her signature and no personal names, just a quickie. Well I wanted more. So there it was: I was going to be a part of the American entourage.

I walked up to the stage door and said to the security man, "Excuse me, has Joan come down? We need to go, it's okay, I'm her make-up artist." He said that no, she hadn't, which meant he believed me. So I acted annoyed, pushed on the door and ran upstairs. It slowly began to dawn on me how crazy this was. What would I actually do when I got to her room? I hadn't thought his through and now I was slightly worried about just how easy this was. I heard noise and laughter, I unrolled my old poster of Joan, I can hear her voice, she's laughing loudly, we meet, I greet her, she greets me, she's very nice, I ask her for her autograph, she signs it, we talk for a bit, I run back downstairs. I say to security, "All is well, she will be down in a sec," and he gives me a nod.

The comedian George Wallace was playing in town and we couldn't afford tickets. I become his American friend, the one he's invited to come to the show. I wait until five minutes before the show starts, I go to the box office knowing full well that you can't disturb the act at this time, and I announce that George has left a pair of tickets for me. They say, "No, he hasn't." I'm feeling like we may have a problem, but it won't be my problem. In the most confident American accent I can manage, I say, "That's okay, but can you tell George he makes no sense! Why would he fly me here and not leave tickets? Tell him I am extremely embarrassed and disappointed, will you tell him that for me please?" I start to walk away and there it is… "Excuse me, we do have a pair of tickets." I thank her, glad I didn't need to cry and start on the baby story. It was a great show.

I've met some phenomenal people. I remember being in Washington DC with Beverley East, the Louise to my Thelma; when we are together, we live an exciting life. We try to get so much done, be it in America, London, or Jamaica. Well this time Tyler Perry was in her town; he was doing a special evening. I said to Beverley, "I love Tyler Perry. I'm going, let's get tickets."

She laughed and said, "There's no way you're going to get into this event, it's been sold out for months, tickets are like gold dust, you just won't get in." Even Beverley thought this was impossible.

"Where there's a will, there's a way…"

She looked at me like she didn't believe I could get into the place. And because she lives in Washington, I began to believe her, but I needed to try, so I said, "Just drop me at that venue." So we get to the venue, and there's this endless queue and I think, *Angie, what are the tricks that you've learned over the years? Come on, girl, get it together.*

I walked up to the venue, looked at the long queue and then the other queue of hopefuls, those without tickets, hoping for returns, but it's not looking like there will be any. They looked at me like, *'Whatever you try has already been done;*

unless you are Oprah right now, it ain't about to happen.' I remember standing there thinking, *'What the mind can conceive, the mind can achieve, I can get in.'*

I stood in the queue with the ticket holders, the better ones, the ones that had got their act together months ago. The queue moved slowly and I moved too and then this woman looks at me, it's as though she could see into my head, she knows that I have no ticket, I'm about to blag something, and she was going to give me a hard time. She's watching me, I have become her project, and she wants to see what I have planned. If I had tickets, I would not look so worried, she can smell the sweat and I know she's thinking, *'She's done this before, I don't like her, she could be a problem.'* I'm thinking, *'I'm getting in there, I'm gonna see Tyler Perry today,'* as I walk up to the ticket section. The woman knows this could all end right here. The woman in front of me goes to the desk and this woman's standing there so I smile at her and she smiles at me. I think, *'You're happy because you have tickets.'*

She said, "Hi, my name is Dale. I have two tickets and my guest isn't coming, so I won't need this one."

"Can I be your guest?" There's nothing like the English accent in America, and being black and British is even better. She said, "Sure you can, honey, I would like that," and she turns to the gate holder and says, "This lovely lady here, she's gonna be my guest." And we walked in together, friends for life. And my old friends were standing outside, watching, thinking, *'She's not getting in…'*

I just lifted my hand, waved, and signalled that I had got in and I would see them later. I went inside with Dale and we quickly became the best of friends. We were walking together because I was her guest now, wasn't I?

Tyler Perry came on and I'm like, *'Oh my God, look at me in front of Tyler Perry with a ticket that isn't mine! I only got in because I wanted to get in.'* It was one of those little moments when life's just fantastic.

You just have to learn to stand in your beliefs because something is going to give. That's why I call it 'standing in my hustle.'

Chapter 25:
The circuit

Doing stand-up was very scary. It was challenging and exciting all at the same time. It felt risky to me. *'I've got this idea in my head and I want to go in front of thousands of people and tell them about it and make them laugh.'* That's risky, right?

It's a lot pressure and it's like that for 20 minutes. If I sang a song, people would clap at the end of it, whether I sang well or not. But the fact that I've told you that you have got to laugh means I am under serious pressure from the get-go. When we started the black comedy club, we laughed so much because we comics were in love with each other; we knew that we were in this together. We were pioneering, we were groundbreaking, we were the first of the black stand-up comics to come forward and say, *'We have a voice, we've got story and you're gonna hear it.'*

Even being the only woman on the bill was never a problem because those guys were like brothers and I'm used to having brothers around me. Those guys on the circuit—Felix Dexter, Jefferson and Whitfield, Leo Chester, Miles Crawford, John Simmit—we'd really built a strong team of people and then we went out and built an audience.

When we first started doing comedy, nobody knew who we were. We had to go out there and build this audience and as people started to recognise us and give us credit, I felt so privileged to be part of it. I could look at what I had done and say, *'Oh my God! I am Britain's first black female comedienne and I'm out there, I'm up and down the roads.'*

A lot of women drop out early with stand-up comedy. They drop out because they have families and they have to travel for work…but women with families, mothers, have another part to play besides that of the joker; they hold a little part of the world, their family. I don't know who's holding the other half but we hold up our end and sometimes you can't help feeling, *'Oh my gosh, how long can I keep going?'*

There were a lot of women that came onto the circuit and dropped off, they joined me and they dropped off, and I was still going, but I knew part of my strength came from my husband because he was doing the driving. When the children were younger, they were in the back of the car. Sometimes people come to the shows and they wonder what's going on behind the scenes. Well behind the scenes for me, there were a couple of kids who were waiting for me to finish the set before driving 200 miles back home.

If it hadn't been for David, I would have dropped out of the stand-up world a lot earlier. Someone says, *'You gotta be in Birmingham, then you gotta be in Bristol, then you gotta be in Manchester'* and you've got all those gigs and you've got to stay in hotels and you've got to stay overnight. That can be scary for a woman, it's very lonely, and it can be dangerous. I got heckled once and I actually came off the stage and went over to the guy thinking I could have it out with him in the audience and he was looking at me like, *'What are you on?'* I'm thinking, *'I'm on something, yes, you're correct.'* He's heckling me; I'm not handling it right. He's getting the better of me so I think of that moment when Oprah's character loses it with Celie in *The Color Purple*. "You told Harpo to beat me… All my life I had to fight." It was one of those moments, and I probably visualised my brothers too. I realised, *'Oh, it's my brothers, I* can fight my brothers but this is an audience member and they're entitled to heckle me.' I walked back onto the stage thinking, '*Did I really just walk off the stage to question this guy? Did I just do that?*' It's at moments like that when you realise how dangerous stand-up can be.

There was another incident too where I got the better of this guy who was heckling me so he jumped onto the stage to fight me. I knew my put down had been sharp because I got a big laugh. I remember looking back at him and he was very angry and embarrassed. Then I saw him getting up. '*Oh no, he's coming towards me*', I thought, and I remember putting the microphone into position, thinking I'm going to have to hit him on the head or something. Then a young lady jumped onto the stage, the host got in the way, and I thought, '*This is a real scary moment.*' But all I could do was fight them as though my brothers were there, just go for it, these things happen. They didn't happen often but they put you off; they can make you think, '*I don't know if this is for me.*'

Heckling is part of it, but you just don't know who is out there. You could upset the wrong person, embarrass them and they're waiting outside for you to tell you they didn't quite like what you said. And you're sitting there trying to negotiate whether or not this is serious or is it going to turn into something nasty…

It wasn't easy. So I really appreciated the support my husband gave me because he was there 90% of the way in terms of moving me around England. I don't think you can do without that, and it's like you look at the work that you do and you go, '*Okay I love this work, but I've got to protect myself too.*'

Those original relationships with the other comics still stand today. There is honesty and respect. I think it's because when we started, we had no idea what we were building, all we knew was we loved this, it was working, and we are being paid for our gift. We willed each other on; we all wanted everyone to have a good gig because it meant the whole event was great. If someone had a bad gig it affected us all. No one person built the black comedy club, we did it together. I don't think it's the same today.

In recent years, we have lost two of our fellow comics: Felix Dexter and Collette Johnson. We all met up for the first time in years at Collette's funeral and that meeting of the Bemarro Sisters inspired us all to talk together again after 25 years apart. That's the thing about death; it's final, you realise that life is too short.

When Felix died, people thought, *'There's no way, that can't be right.'* I got a text saying my friend was in hospital dying, and I thought it was a bad joke. When we got that text, it was like, *'Surely not Felix? He can't die, he's a great comic. How could he die?'* I actually had those ignorant thoughts and then we contacted his family and it was true, he only had about three or four more weeks. So a friend and I went to the hospice to see him and we sat there and something about him didn't look sick at all because he was still very funny. And he was still cracking jokes. It felt weird because I knew he was dying. He sounded like he knew he was dying too but at same time he was saying, "When I come out, I've got a few things I've got to get sorted out."

I asked him how he was with God and he said, "I'm thinking about that, I'm thinking." I don't know what made me say that, but I felt I had to. I know people are sensitive about their spirituality; I wasn't there to push it. I just wanted to leave it there.

The love for Felix was awesome to see. When I saw the social media networks and what people were saying about him and how they felt about him and what he meant to them, I realised how much love was out there for him. It was well deserved. The BBC did a special for him on BBC2, which is unheard of, especially for somebody who didn't have their own TV show, but Felix was loved so much. It was great that the BBC did the tribute as they didn't really give him what I think he deserved. A lot of people also felt it deeply, but it also reminded me that we are all going to die, and what do we want people to say about us, how do we want to impact their lives? Are we important enough to get a surge on the social media networks? I think it's okay just to have close loved ones and no surge.

When Felix died, we were broken. Felix Dexter was a kind gentleman and so funny, and he will never be forgotten.

This funny bone gift can turn on you at any time. I've been booed, cheered, had standing ovations, the lot. There were many times when I thought, *'Angie, why don't you just get a nine-to-five job and stop putting yourself under this intense pressure?'*

I was booked to perform at the 291 Club, which was similar to the American show *Live at the Apollo*. If you were no good, you'd get booed off. *'Well, I'm a guest,'* I thought, *'There's nothing to worry about, I've been booked, I'm a special guest.'* Two minutes into my set, I was being booed. It started in the front row, I was heckled by some girls. They shouted out, "You think you're too nice," and I cheekily responded, "Well what am I thinking now?" They got it eventually, and then it started, and that encouraged the whole audience. I got my full pay for two minutes' work. As I got into my car to drive home, I was still a bit shaken. I'd had this great 20-minute set, and here I was driving home, upset, tears falling. I felt embarrassed, ashamed, and just a little bit disappointed that I hadn't been able to turn it around and win the crowd back.

Thank the Lord we didn't have Twitter and Facebook then, that could have got trending. Luckily for me, we were living in normal times, so it was just a rumour for a bit and then it went away. Or I could be stupid enough to write it down in a book and tell all those who never even knew that I was booed…

Chapter 26:
This show business

I had been doing the circuit for years with my friends the Bemarro Sisters and not much was happening. We were gigging, we were performing, and it was just going backwards and forwards. Before we split, there was a TV show being cast called *The Real McCoy*. We heard that they were coming down to this theatre, the Albany Empire, and they were looking at talent. We felt that we were so ready for this; this was going to be our big break. We didn't know when the producers were coming in; we didn't know what was going to happen. We just knew that somebody was going to be out there in the audience over the next couple of days for the show that we were doing, and we should be cast in that TV show. It was going to be the British version of *In Living Color*. It was the break that most black comedians were waiting for and then all of a sudden we found out that the show had been cast and we hadn't got a call. I was floored. *"Surely I should have had a call? Surely I am one of the leading black female comedienne right now. I should have gotten that call."*

There was a lot of resentment and a lot of bitterness because when the show came out, it was the show that everybody was talking about. And whilst everybody was talking about the show, everybody was asking me why I wasn't on it, and I was getting fed up with explaining why I was not in the show. "I am not in it, no big deal, now just leave me alone."

So now when I watch the show, although I'm laughing my head off, I can't see anything funny in it. The show was hilarious, but I was so disappointed… I really wanted to be in that show. And it was consuming me. There was an interview I did. I must have said something snide about it like, *"Oh well, they didn't hold auditions anyway."* It was that feeling you have when there is scarcity. What? Black people on telly? It was like I'd missed the train to heaven, and although there was a strong chance that another would come in time, it probably wouldn't be for another decade or so. It was what I'd worked for, but I wasn't good enough. I wasn't considered as one of the good black comics. Boy, it hurt.

I just got on with my life; I continued to write to Lenny Henry, and Lenny Henry didn't respond; I knew I wasn't getting past his agents. Lenny was our leading black comedian, maybe he could help. I continued with my life and I continued watching the show and thinking to myself, *'It is good, but it would have been better if I'd been in it.'* Then a friend of mine, Treva Etienne, was called to produce the show. I think it was the fourth series and they had introduced a stand-up section which I thought was a good idea. He contacted me and asked, "Angie, will you do a stand-up section?"

I said, "I can't because the cast doesn't like me. I think I upset them in the press."

"Don't be silly, Angie, that's not true. You have to do it. It would be a great break for you."

"I can't! I don't want anything to do with the show. My time has gone."

I did the show. I remember walking into the studio and going to my changing room. There was a bit of tension, and I told myself, *'You've got five minutes to smash this, and you'd better smash this because a lot of people don't want this to work.'* I had rehearsed my lines back to back; I knew where the jokes were coming and I knew exactly what I was going to do. I went out there and smashed it.

The next day, everybody was talking about Angie's performance. To this day, everybody thinks I was in the whole series and all I did was five minutes. But it did bring me to the attention of the Channel 4 show *Get Up Stand Up*. Being on *The Real McCoy* and not getting my break drew attention from another producer called Malcolm Frederick. He called me up and said, "Angie, I think it's time for you to do TV."

I remember thinking, '*Thank you so much, Malcolm,*' because I needed a TV break. I had been through a lot of theatre and you need TV to push the theatre just a little bit more or you could just end up disappearing. I was truly grateful.

So this was perfect for me. Channel 4 sat down with its writers; we had lots of writers on board because this was new. We were going to go on location, a lot of shows were in the studio, and the budget was big. Malcolm said to me, "You are going to make a lot of money and whatever you do, save it, don't squander it."

That was the best advice that he gave me. I put it into bricks and built a house. When the work dries up, at least you have a home and I still say, '*Thank you, Malcolm.*'

We did four years on that show and it was really good for me. It helped me as a writer, as an actress and made me understand this business. Imagine working alongside legends you'd grown up with, Malcolm Frederick and Chris Tummings, who were from the hit 80s sitcom *No Problem*. Every day was like a special day. I used to have a crush on Chris' character; Toshiba was his name back then, so it took me a while to get used to him asking me, "What you having for lunch, Ang? Let's go out." They truly guided me through that series; it was like having two older brothers on hand, every step of the way.

It was one of those shows that boosted my career and from there I started getting more TV work, late night hosting, guest panellist, that kind of thing. Everything was moving quite nicely.

I then got asked on to do the comedy sitcom *Birds of a Feather*. Just when you are riding mighty and high, something will come along and knock you down and put you back in your place again. I remember the night: I was sitting around the table with my family and friends to watch my episode of *Birds of a Feather*. I'm waiting for my bit to come on. My character walks on, but it was another actress. For a moment, I forced myself to look at her, there was a resemblance… But then I had to accept defeat. It wasn't me, it was my worst nightmare: I'd been replaced. My mum looked at me, like, *'Why are we here again?'* I felt so ridiculous, simply because I hadn't known. I had no understanding about the way things were done. *'Wasn't I good enough? Did I not come across?'* All of this was racing through my head as everybody started to leave, looking at me like, *'Are you sure you were there, or were you just fantasising?'* Then the looks of disappointment, *'You did your best but somehow your best wasn't good enough.'*

I found out later that I didn't look old enough and the role had to be replaced. I'd told the local press that I was going to be on *Birds of a Feather*…the local girl's done good and all of that. But then I wasn't there. And even though you have success going on around you, those moments bring you down to ground zero. You think, *'Oh my word, this business is quite awkward, depressing, and at times very harsh.'* My ego was so out of place and I felt so embarrassed. But in those situations, all you can do is get back on the horse and make yourself see it as a minor blip.

There were constant talks of me having my own show. I mean, I had a network of producers sitting me down and saying, "Angie, we want to give you your own show, you have built a great reputation for yourself and a huge black audience, but can you make white people laugh?"

I would say, "If they have a sense of humour, I can."

I believe that humour has no colour; you either get it or you don't.

Chapter 27:
Take a bow

I had no idea that I would have great success in the theatre world. That world can be a little snobbish at times, and I felt it; I knew I wasn't going to fit into that world. At times, I felt that maybe it wasn't for me. I found it a little anal if I'm honest. *Funny Black Women* gave me such confidence because I was writing what I wanted to see, I wanted to write roles that I wanted to audition for. The audience was in agreement with me; they wanted to see it too. After the success of *Funny Black Women on the Edge*, I enrolled in many writing courses; I needed to know what I was missing, I wanted to get it right.

Tyler Perry has been a huge inspiration for me, selling out a 3,000 seater theatre in Los Angeles with *The Diary of a Mad Black Woman*, watching his set rotate like I hadn't seen in London in black productions, the slick presentation, it all stuck with me. I know his shows were big productions, but nonetheless I also wanted to present stylish plays.

Later on in life when I was ill, I remember praying to God and saying, '*God, if I get better, I promise to listen to you. Please tell me what I need to do. I'm tired of the rejection; the doors that I'm knocking don't seem to be opening. I feel as though there is a block and I can't get through it.*'

I don't know why there was a block on me, but I did feel ignored. I remember being told by a friend, who was sitting in at a big TV meeting for a new comedy show, that they said my name and another friend said to the enthusiastic TV executives, "No, not Angie Le Mar, she's too much of a troublemaker." I was so shocked, upset, and hurt. I mean, this women was a friend...I guess.

A reporter once called me, very upset. She'd just interviewed a well-known director and was shocked at his response when she mentioned *Funny Black Women* and its phenomenal success. The director said, "We need to do away with shows like that and get back to proper theatre."

So I wasn't making this feeling of rejection up in my head, was I?

I just had to keep on going. I remember God saying to me clearly, "You need to cut out the middlemen and go STRAIGHT TO YOUR AUDIENCE. You keep asking them for the permission to be great, but I have already made you great." Okay, God, I hear you loud and clear! I formed Straight to Audience Productions in 2000. It was alive and active, let's go, God!

An American soap drama called *The Young and the Restless* inspired *The Brothers*. My mum was a big fan of that show. Anytime I was in Jamaica, where my parents had moved to by then, she'd switch it on at 7 pm every evening. She never missed an episode; her body clock was wired to sound the alarm at 7 pm. You could be in a deep conversation with her and at 7 pm she'd cut you off mid-sentence to go and watch her programme. I tried it a few times and she would always shut down at 7 pm, you just couldn't speak to her until *The Young and the Restless* was over.

I wondered if I could do something like that, I wanted to test it. I was on radio at the time; I wanted to see if I could stop people at a certain time with a radio drama. I'd tested one out before, *Sharp Cuts*. I wanted to write something that would bring in the listeners.

I spoke with my producer, Ivor. He was inspired by this idea and *The Brothers* was born. I wanted to write about black men who weren't into the drugs and negativity that we were constantly fed about them. I wanted to show that we have men in our community who deal with everyday issues just like every other man out there, the same relationship issues, friendships, betrayals, just normal things, no guns, no knives, but educated brothers who are doing well and living a stylish life.

I called in a few friends to do the voices for me and Ivor produced the shows. We all worked so well together. The show took off straightaway; the ratings for that slot on my show were going through the roof. We had thousands and thousands of new listeners, that slot for ten minutes was the peak of my whole show; it was clear, the audience had spoken, we had a hit!

Then God spoke again, "Do it as a play." It was the easiest transfer. I adapted the radio play for theatre while it was still at an early stage. I did a test run; I worked out the actors and the script, in a smaller section of the Hackney Empire. It sold out for two weeks. It was time to mount the show in the main theatre; this meant some recasting had to take place because some of the actors were not strong enough for the main space. It was a difficult decision, I know that it hurt a few of the actors, but it was a decision we had to make; we needed stronger actors with names to take on the demands of the main space. It's really nice when you can give an actor a break, but letting actors go, or holding auditions, when people feel you should have given them that role is always the awkward bit. To this day, a few of the actors still don't speak to me. But what can you do apart from explain? It was nothing personal.

The Brothers opened with actors Chucky Venn, Richard Blackwood and Nolan Weekes. It was the fastest-selling show at the Hackney Empire, bar Ralph Fiennes' *Hamlet*. We completely smashed the box office and returned with a few more runs. We sold out again and had to add midnight shows to deal with the demand.

I was sitting in the dress circle one afternoon and I looked at the stage and said to God, *'I get it, take charge of my destiny; no one is going to give this to me. I have to take it.'*

The reviews were awesome, but even great reviews don't always sell a show. Word of mouth sells a show faster than any review. I saw audiences get on their mobiles phones in the interval and call their friends, saying, "You need to get your tickets, it's wicked!" Job done.

One night I was called to the box office to meet the security guards who were with a group of young boys, a gang of hooded up little stereotypes. They had sneaked into the theatre to watch *The Brothers*. They said they were looking for their teacher but they couldn't remember her name or the name of the school, they had forgotten that too. The security guards were about to send them out, but I was so impressed that they'd sneaked into a theatre to watch a play that I couldn't let them go. Who knows, one of them could have been the next Idris Elba! I said, "They can go on my guest list." They ran inside, the hoodies came down, they smiled at me and said thank you.

We followed up the show with an *MTV Base* recording which was aired on TV. It continued to smash the ratings; they repeated the life out of that recording.

The next play I wrote was *Forty*. Maya Angelou said it beautifully, "We are more alike than we are unalike" and this was the premise behind *Forty*. It was about friends meeting up after 25 years apart. I wanted to present different types of black women; I was excited by this play, I wanted to see a different portrayal of black women.

Sometimes I wonder if we will always struggle with this issue in the UK… They say the first rule of writing is to write what you know. Well then if this is true, you are going to write about me through the eyes of the media, through the stereotypes. I'm not going to be the star; I'm just not in the forefront of your mind. That's okay; we can write our own stories. The power is in the pen. No one is going to do us justice unless we write our own story, and that was my point. I have been so blessed with my audience, who without knowing, encouraged me to keep going; they pushed me to write and deliver.

There have been times when my audience feels they can tell me their thoughts. One audience member complained about *Forty*, she felt there was too much swearing in it. I went through the script; she was right so I cut some out. One woman called me and said she hated *Forty*, every bit of it. I was shocked at what she was telling me, she was really angry with me, then I had to say to her, "Okay, I get that you didn't like the play, but back up a bit, I can't please everyone, and I understand that that's the business."

I felt something else was going on as she wanted to keep talking. After a few questions, she shared that she was reaching 40 soon and the play had brought up too many issues to deal with, so she was angry with me, she felt I had touched a nerve. We spoke at length, she was scared of the future, she hadn't achieved her goals, and she felt she was running out of time. She thought my play would have been a lovely celebration of arriving at 40, but instead my characters were dealing with domestic violence, affairs, sexual identity, and some real old pain that they'd caused each other in their earlier years.

After we talked a while longer, we laughed and I wished her the best. She told me that really she loved the play, but she was angry with herself. Thankfully I don't get calls like that too often.

The cast of *Do You Know Where Your Daughter is?* This production was inspired by a phone call on my Choice FM radio show, a young girl discussing how she was abused by her boyfriend. I wanted the play to open debate around our daughters. We toured London schools, colleges and theatres, and finally Edinburgh Fringe Festival.

Daughters cast. L-R (above)Tyler Whyte, Tara Brown, Claire Butler, Sophia Sinclair, Naomi J Lewis, plus Aaron Fontaine, Victoria Evaristo, Orlessa Altass, Vicki Elliot, Maria Simmond and Peter Bakare.

The cast of *Funny Black Women on the Edge:* Yvette Rochester-Duncan, Chizzy Akudolu, Petra Letang, Josephine Melville

The many cast of *Funny Black Women on the Edge* over the years.

The Brothers: actors Chucky Venn, Richard Blackwood
and Nolan Weekes.

The Brothers, the fastest selling show. We returned with other actors,
such as Jason Barrett and Harvey, a huge success.

The cast of the play *Forty*, five friends who meet for the first time in 25 years.
L-R Orlessa Altass, Carol Moses, myself, Ellen O'Grady, and the late
Catherine Hammond RIP.

The cast of *The Ryan Sisters* sitcom - Somalia Seaton, Tanya Moodie and
Ellen Thomas.

Channel 4 show *Get Up Stand Up* with Malcolm Frederick
and Chris Cummings

With director Femi Elufowoju Jr. for rehearsals of *In My Shoes*

I finally got Lenny Henry! He came to see *In My Shoes* at the Soho Theatre; truly inspired by his thoughts and feedback.

In My Shoes. Some characters from the show.

The gazebo at my parents' home in Jamaica, my writing spot.

Chapter 28:
Is this my time?

The cutting of my locs was quite a significant event. Was it symbolic of a new beginning? A regrowth maybe? I had always wanted to locs my hair because I couldn't do it when I was a child. Not that I wanted to as a child but it was not an option in a Christian home to locs your hair or consider becoming a Rasta. Not that I wanted to be Rasta, but to locs my hair was something that I just always wanted to do.

When I fell pregnant with my last child, my parents had already gone to Jamaica. I had two young boys and I felt that was going to be my lot because my parents had been the hidden support system that had allowed me and my husband to work. Whilst doing what we were doing, my parents were helping me. We were raising the children; they picked them up from the schools, those last minute drop-offs when I had to rush to a meeting or an audition, or perhaps the odd party. So when they went to Jamaica for good, it didn't make sense to be thinking of having another child.

But as soon as they went, I got pregnant. I just couldn't believe it. I went to my doctors and I was talking about not knowing what to do, being confused about having a child. It was a new doctor, an African, one who was standing in for my normal doctor, and I was just talking to him. Because he wasn't my usual doctor, I think I could be open with him about being in a bad space and not thinking I could cope. He told me the story of his wife who had a daughter. She didn't want to be pregnant, but then she realised that she had to have the child because that was what she was supposed to do. The doctor told me she'd been in exactly the same place I was in and that they now had a lovely and beautiful daughter and his wife was happy.

I said, "Thank you very much for telling me your story, but that's your story and not my story. My family is not here; my mum is not here, and I don't know how to do this without her."

When I was growing up, I didn't think I'd have children. I had a feeling that I would be this famous actress who lived in the heart of the West End in a lovely apartment looking over the River Thames—location was important—I had to be in the heart of theatreland. Of course, it didn't quite work out like that.

I went home and cried; I was pregnant and feeling low, I was feeling very low. My husband couldn't understand what the problem was; it was just another child, he knew we could cope. Then I thought, *'With support from family and friends, it's all good; I can get on with it. It's not like I haven't had children before, I can do this.'*

I suffered from migraines throughout the pregnancy. These were headaches that painkillers were not going to ease; it was a pain that would make you want to harm yourself. I went to the doctors and they didn't know what it was so they gave me paracetamol. I was in so much pain. I thought I was dying.

Late one evening, I was driving home feeling dreadful and the pain was getting worse. I just wanted to get home, get in my bed, and be still; it was like something vicious was pouring into my head. I started to lose the vision on my right side, it went just like that. I couldn't get home. I pulled over and called my husband: "Dave, I can't see, I can't see!" I was scared, I was panicking; *'I'm losing my sight'*. I curled up in my car, waiting for Dave. I was scared to open my eyes as it was getting darker and darker.

I was rushed to hospital. After checking me over, there was a surreal moment when the doctor, who looked very concerned, said in a serious voice, "We think it's a brain tumour." I looked at my husband and then I looked away. He was trying to be strong and I remember thinking, *'They will have to shave my hair, and that means I can't put my weave on. How can they sew it on if there's no hair?'* Silly thoughts like these were the only relief from the tumour thought; I sat there thinking, "A tumour, that's a bit much."

I had an MRI scan and they found that my brain was being crushed by water. All the fluid from my pregnancy was going to my brain. So where the pressure was supposed to be about 15, it was actually 52. The water was crushing my brain and the back of my eye, and that's why the sight went.

I had to have a lumbar puncture pretty much every other week throughout my pregnancy. The thing with lumbar punctures is that if you have to have one, it's usually just the one. It's not a procedure to repeat lightly because it's so dangerous: the needle has to go into the spine. But for me, it was every other week. It would drain the fluid from my brain, but it would leave a very dry headache. It was almost as bad as the water pressure headache until the fluid covered it up a bit.

That was the worst time in my life, and I thought, *'God, would you take me? This is taking too long. I can't do this all the way through this pregnancy; it's just killing me.'*

So because my parents were in Jamaica, my mother-in-law, who I didn't get on with then, decided to come and look after me because my husband had to work. I dreaded it so much and wondered how I was going to get along with her when I was sick. But it was one of the closest bonding experiences I have ever had because it was all about love, about her looking after me. She wasn't there to have an issue with me, because you know mother-in-laws and their sons, and it just wasn't about that.

"You are sick and your mother is not here, so I am kicking in." She kicked in and looked after me. The most my husband could do was wash me in bed and take me to and from the hospital to drain the fluid off.

I read a book at that time called *Conversations with God*. I said, *"I was raised in the church, and I am going to talk to you. Why am I going through this? Is it my time? I don't think I've finished what I was supposed to do."*

My mum flew in from Jamaica nearer the baby's due date. They told me the baby was going to be born on March 26, but I was not allowed to go into labour because that would kill me instantly. My daughter was born was February 27. They gave me the wrong date; if I had gone by that date, I would have gone into labour and died.

Mum knew. She walked in, looked at me and told my husband, "Take her to the hospital now."

"Mum, I am not ready to go to the hospital, I am just going to lie down."

"David, take her to the hospital now."

When I got to the hospital, they rushed me in and took the baby out. My mother looked into my eyes afterwards and said, "No, something ain't right."

There wasn't a bright time; it was grey, everything was dull, it was quiet, and it was still. If you looked into my eyes, you would see sickness. My mother had to look into my eyes to see the sickness because only she would be able to tell.

My boys have names beginning with T: Travis and Tyler. I wanted another T name for my daughter. I was going to call her Toni, but while I was sleeping, I had a dream about this little girl at the bottom of the bed. I asked her what her name was. She had a head of hair and she was wearing a yellow dress. She said, "My name is True."

I woke up and told David. "Her name is True, the baby's name is True." When I told my friend, she said, "Take off the 'e', just keep it Tru," and that was it. So her full name (because my husband's name is Prosper) is Tru Prosper.

When I got back from hospital, I knew my life was going to change. The hardest thing for me was that my phone didn't ring as much as I thought it would. I didn't have as many friends as I thought I did. I understand people's lives go on, but it was so quiet.

Brenda Emmanus, the TV presenter, who has been my dear friend for many years, showed up for me. What a great friend she is! She used to live over the road from the hospital and she would make herself available for me, even though she had such an extremely busy schedule. She was always home for me when I needed her. After yet another lumbar puncture, I would go over to her house to rest and wait for my husband, who would pick me up later in the evening.

The friends who I thought would notice that I was missing…well, they didn't. I kept saying to people, "Didn't you notice that I disappeared for over a year?" I was a bit nervous about getting back out there, I remember going back on the circuit and my confidence was so low. One promoter booked me to do a show and I was so grateful and humble; I couldn't understand why he was excited to have me in his show. I was very sick, my confidence was at an all-time low, and I charged him a low price because I was so grateful.

On the night, I smashed it and had a great show. The promoter said, "Angie, would you mind if I gave you more money?"

"Why would you do that?"

"Because you're Angie Le Mar and you're getting the smallest amount of money on this bill. Everybody's getting more than you and I can't do that to you."

I was like, *"Oh my God, is my confidence so low that I don't even know how to price myself?"* I was so moved by his kindness, he didn't have to do that, I was just glad to be on the circuit again. It wasn't even about money; I wanted to know if I was still funny or if my illness had taken away any of my comedic timing. No. I hadn't lost it, the timing was firmly intact.

My confidence was shot. Coming back from illness and the pregnancy, coming back onto the circuit, coming from a sick place and not knowing where you are…when you are at death's door, you don't want to play around any more and you want to do things seriously. But my confidence wasn't up for it ye,t and it took me about a year to take off the weight and get back to being confident Angie Le Mar.

Chapter 29:
Fifty

When I was growing up, getting to 50 years old felt like a huge task. From my naïve teenage point of view, it seemed so far away and looked really old. It had the smell of Deep Heat, joints ached, a little bit of arthritis was starting to set in...

It's cute to be asked your age at 21, you say it with a lot of pride, the same goes for 30. As you get into your forties, you start to question people's motives. We are told that life begins at 40, okay, well that's nice... Forty was hard work for me, it's like I needed to start getting my life right because I was getting old. I needed to hurry up and sort out my relationships because my biological clock was almost done, there was an alarm set to go off soon and it was going to be loud!

The career that you've been procrastinating about, come on, get on with it, you're getting old, and the younger generation is snapping at your heels, the younger, cooler, and technically minded, they are very savvy and they are coming! My God, they are marching towards us, they have great ideas, they're already making money, the things you're still going for, they've got. My God, they are great! You have inspired them, don't forget, they were watching you. You can't stay in the same place, because they are coming for it, RUN!!!

They said 40 is the new 30 but that's just to make us feel good. No, 40 is 40, you may look great for your age, but you are your age. Let's be grateful and stop this lie, it's a lie that will slow you down. Nowhere else in society do they let you off, mortgage lenders don't say, *'Well 40 is the new 30, let's add that to their working years.'* When you start sweating because the menopause IS on its way, you may look great but your body has a brief to stick to and it needs to get on with the work. Your hot flushes will be on time, please prepare and act accordingly.

As you know, I didn't plan all my pregnancies. If I had done, maybe I would have waited, or even started to panic in my forties. Today when I look at my family photos, I think, *'WOW,'* because that wasn't my plan, nature took its course, I trusted it and went with it. It could have been a completely different story.

The conversation changes as you get older, women may have talked about periods and pregnancies, but now it's fibroids and nothing prepares you for the fibroids… We talk over a glass of wine about how to deal with hot flushes at work; that's when you know you're in the big girls' group. You find your people at seminars instead of raves, at yoga classes, swimming. I swim every day and my swimming friends are like my dog friends who only recognise me when I'm with my dog. My swimming friends only see me naked, well, swimwear is almost naked; when I have my clothes on, they walk past me. I have to run up to them and tear open my shirt and say, *'It's me.'*

Yes, black women do swim, come to my pool, we are there in numbers getting our hair wet; we are the older lot though. I wear a swimming hat over my hair, and then put a wig on, yes, I know, my wig can get wet and take on all the damage, I'm happy, my hair is dry. I don't look great with a swimming hat on its own, I look out of balance without my hair, I look very rounded, with a bean head, it's okay, this is not low self-esteem talking, it just is what it is. However, when I'm in the changing room, I have to time when I'm taking it off because the wig coming off is too much for people, and then I'm standing there with a blue cap, it's hard to process. Once this lady watched me, she stared at me, and then she looked at me as if to say, *'I understand.'* It's my thing, it works.

Every January, *Essence Magazine* would dedicate a special issue to the women in their fifties and upwards, sometimes into their nineties. I found it the most inspirational piece of journalism. Why? It gave me hope. These beautiful women would share their testimonies, their beautiful stories about how they lived their lives, the healthy eating habits, the long walks, and their spirituality. Awesome.

When I reached 40, life didn't begin, it continued. I tried to throw it all in the air, but a few things came tumbling down as if to say, *'Angie, you may need these, you ain't there yet.'* I didn't feel rebellious, I felt under pressure. In my eyes, by 40 I should have been at the Academy tearfully receiving my award. I'd hold up the award and say, "I just want to say thank you to my loving parents, I couldn't have done this without you. My family and friends, you have supported me and my dreams, you are truly..." Pause... A few tears, nearly choked. Back to script. "...wonderful and kind. Thank you. Steven Spielberg, you believed in me, that special audition when you allowed me to be my dyslexic self, thank you. But my special thanks goes to my God, Father God, thank you." I leave the stage with Oprah, we laugh together, because, you see, at this stage in my life, Oprah is actually my good friend, we've been friends for years. Of course, Gayle is happy with this, it was Gayle I met first and she said, *'Oprah would love you!'* She was right! We ALL hang together, they never leave me out.

That's what my fortieth was supposed to look like. I had planned that from my twenties so excuse me, when you say life begins at 40, I'm thinking, *'You're late.'*

As the years went on, I started to get it; it does begin. It begins to take shape; you begin to work out who you truly are. I think in my forties, I started to accept that it's not over; it's a journey, a place you don't actually get to. I get it, you just keep moving and you keep fixing, loving, hurting, and forgiving. The difference is your experience; you deal with things differently, you stop beating yourself up for your mistakes and the mistakes of others, you are no longer consumed with old pain; you learn to forgive and let go.

The understanding of forgiveness is such a breakthrough. Realising that when you forgive, you are not letting those who hurt you off, you are allowing yourself to move on. I used to think, *'If they haven't said sorry, how can I forgive them?'* The power of forgiveness is truly awesome; it just helps you move on. Thank you, Oprah, those many TV interviews were not wasted, we did get it.

As I was approaching 50, a little panic started to set in. Had I done enough? How come I still don't feel like a grown up? How come the Academy hasn't called? Then you calm down without even noticing it, you realise that the focus is not you. If you are blessed to still have your parents and your siblings with you, if your children and husband are alive and healthy, well you find the entries in your gratitude diary change. The things that used to matter don't. So the producers didn't call back, or you didn't get that big contract. Right now, your parents need you, your thoughts are elsewhere. One day you just don't feel desperate anymore. There's this sense of, *'If it's for me, it cannot go by me.'*

My father used to phone me every day from Jamaica. "Just checking on you," he'd say. If he called and I wasn't there, he got concerned about where I was. I used to find myself trying to schedule my days to receive those calls. They were more important to me than any call from the Academy.

You attend a few of your school friends' funerals and you can't help but think, *'But they weren't old, they had so much to live for.'* You look around and see their lost and broken families; you have to leave feeling blessed and incredibly grateful for life and your loved ones.

I loved the time in which I was born. I feel so sad for the youth today. When we were growing up, we went to parties and bad things could happen, maybe a little argument broke out, but we were there to party and we had no fear of being killed, of brutal fights and gang life. Today, I am always worrying about my children and today's youth and the low price that's put on life. It seems mad to want material things when spiritually we are so out of sync.

On the eve of my fiftieth birthday, I stared for a long time at that number thinking, *'That number doesn't even suit me, the shape is nice but it isn't me.'* It was still over there in the Deep Heat pile. On the morning, I gave God thanks for fifty years. I looked in the mirror and thought, *'I don't feel like a 50-year-old, I don't look it, or maybe I do, who knows what it should look like.'* That evening, I partied with my family and friends. I wasn't going to celebrate it at first, but then it was clear that this was a milestone, I'm still standing, still dreaming, I have more plans and aspirations. I am excited by life, the life that I have lived and the life I continue to live.

Here's to another fifty years.

Celebrating my fiftieth with friend Grace Ononiwu OBE and businessman Tim Campbell.

Behind the scenes of *An Audience With Angie Le Mar*
L-R Queen of UK Gospel Lurine Cato, comedienne Tameka Empson,
myself and Joycelyn Gee, showing great support on the night.

Media friends Diane Parish, Michelle Matherson, Brenda Emmnaus,
myself, Sherry A Dixon and Dionne Grant.

Dionne Grant and Akosua Annobil, the ladies behind the voices supporting me on my Saturday morning show at Choice FM, bringing the stories and gossip and a whole lot more.

My dear friend Brenda Emmanus, who has truly been there through the tough times.

Chapter 30:
Daddy's girl

I am a daddy's girl through and through, and I always knew my dad loved me; even when he was silent, there was pure love pouring out of him.

My dad died at 6.27 am on 16th April 2016. I'd just stepped out of the room and he was slipping away but I caught him in time. Wow, Dad! Just like that. But he was ready; he'd had a great life and it was now time to go.

My life will never be the same again. My dad was no ordinary dad; he was my friend, my advisor and my personal cheerleader. My heart aches as I write about him in past tense.

As a little girl, I spent my life saying, "my dad, my dad, my dad" or, "I'm telling my dad," "my dad will give me the money for that doll," "my dad will pick me up," "my dad will take care of it," and he always did. My dad could do anything, there was nothing he wouldn't do for me, and during those final days of his life, as difficult as they were, I felt so blessed that I was in Jamaica to be by his bedside, day and night, nursing him, feeding him, praying with him until the end.

He would say, "The big switch is imminent, prepare yourself, Angie. I'm going home to be with my Lord." When I slept over at Hargreaves Hospital with him, I would hear him at night saying, "Merciful Father, take me home." Then in the morning, I'd say, "You're still here, Dad, God isn't ready."

My parents returned home to live in their much loved homeland, Jamaica, after 35 years in England. It was their hearts' desire. We grew up knowing they wanted to return one day, so it was no surprise when that day came. But nothing can prepare you for that container arriving for their furniture; it made my heart sink as I watched them empty their whole home of its contents, all their possessions just boxed up, homeward bound.

My dad was truly at peace back in Jamaica; now his stories had the picturesque backdrop that I had heard about so many times. My parents' home was surrounded by palm trees, and they stood strong, pretty as a Caribbean postcard, the hot sun shining down on their dream. I have never seen so much land, different sections with different roles, the upper front veranda where we had our breakfast each morning, the lower front veranda, the back garden fit for cultivation, full with yams and cassava waiting the time to be dug up, potatoes, pumpkin, the health-filled noni. There was fruit everywhere, mouth-watering mangos and towering coconut trees, just waiting for someone to climb them so we could crack one open and drink. We would taste this special water that goes straight to your heart, the only water that will do that, my dad told me. The front garden had a very special design. There were flower beds filled with a fusion of colours; the lawn was precisely laid with a stylish concrete table and chair set. I was impressed: this garden had everything, two large banana trees, several ackee trees, orange trees, a guinep tree. For the first time in my life, I saw pomegranates hanging from a small tree. I knew my dad loved horses and dogs, but 12 barking dogs seemed a bit much. They were fierce, they would rush around the house barking and wagging their tails, keeping the house and land secure. This is the home that they'd spent years building, the beautiful dream home now had its residents.

The gazebo became such a special place for us as a family. It was such a beautiful design, built on a water tank, which had the capacity to store a lot of water, with a place to relax built over it. It was so idyllic that it was the perfect place for me to make my marriage vows to David. My father was emotional as he gave me away. My dad walking with me to the gazebo was a perfect moment. I had tears in my eyes as I held onto him; he was so happy, his chest was bursting with pride. At the wedding reception, he said to Dave, "Dave, I'm not giving her to you, I'm loaning her to you, and I will never give her away."

I was so glad for that day. I'd often said I wouldn't get married unless my dad was there to give me away. Well he did and the memories will be treasured forever.

The gazebo became the perfect writing spot for me. My plays, *The Brothers, Do you know where your daughter is?* and *Forty*, were inspired and written there. I stayed up there for hours, thinking, reading and working things out, taking the occasional break with my dad. He always brought two freshly peeled oranges for me, then he would make sure the hammock was steady, strengthening it, making sure his slightly overweight daughter didn't burst through it, and yes, I did a few times, the strings would give out. I knew it was my fault, but my dad always made it seem as though the manufacturers were the ones at fault.

My dad promised never to return to England and I could understand why; his home was perfect, he had dreamt of this all his life. He did return though, but that was for a sad occasion, a difficult time, when he came to say goodbye to his beloved brother, our special and wonderful Uncle Tee. They were two brothers who truly loved each other. They were like two peas in a pod; they would spend endless evenings talking about the cricket. One of my dad's favourite pastimes was talking about the Windies, the West Indian cricket team. I knew he missed playing the game. The laughter as they discussed what Garfield Sobers was doing and how that was an LBW from Viv Richards to Clive Lloyd. We heard their support, but it was Brian Lara claiming another century that would have us running into the front room to find out what all the shouting and cheering about.

Being around my dad was always my aim as a child. If he was going out, as long as it wasn't to church, I was going with him. Sitting in the front seat of the Triumph 2000, and after that one, the silver Volvo Estate, that was my dream. I followed him everywhere. My dad loved his cars. My first car was a Sunbeam which I was delighted to get for £200. He just looked at it and said, "That car has about £200 worth of driving in it." He was right. It wasn't too long later that I had to call him late at night, "Daddy, why does my car have all this black smoke coming out of the engine?"

My dad would share stories about when he first came to the UK, the sadness he felt, and how much he missed his wife. He had only planned to stay a year, make enough money to buy a truck, and then return to Jamaica so he could continue his work with his new truck. I found the stories about his early days in Britain painfully sad; my dad was one of the new wave of immigrants who had arrived in the early 60s to rebuild a better Britain. Britain's brutal winters were hard for him; I could feel how cold he'd been when he described how his hands had often been so frozen that he could cry. The cold was hard to deal with and so were the unwelcoming racist people. But things got easier when his wife arrived a year later.

My dad learned his trade as an electrician and for years worked on the first team of electricians at the London Weekend Building, known as the LWT Building. Later he started his own company, Martins Electricals, which he ran until he retired. Many times I answered calls and wrote the wrong numbers down because my dyslexic brain couldn't process the speed at which people gave me their numbers. Then the strangest thing would happen; when my dad told me the number was wrong, I always found I could dial the right number straightaway. My brain remembered it, it was just that I wrote something completely different. There were times when my dad would just say, "Angie, just ring the number for me, save time."

My dad rewired so many homes and his reputation was excellent. Even years later when he was back home in Jamaica, customers would ring to see if he was still be available for work.

I spent many years listening to friends and women talk about their fathers. Call me naïve, but I honestly thought everyone's Dad was like my dad. My close friends had great dads too so I thought it was normal. But as I got older, I heard so many horror stories… I understood that I was truly blessed to have this wonderful man as my father.

I could always rely on my dad; he'd pick me up from drama club every Wednesday and Friday at 9 pm, never late. My dad was never late and truly hated people who couldn't keep time. If my dad said jump, I would ask "How high?" This was a man who everybody loved and trusted. I remember when I thought I was a big woman and applied for a flat after I had Travis. The council gave me a flat on the 23rd floor and my dad came to see it. He looked out the windows and said, "Even birds don't fly this high." So I had to tell the council, "No, I'm not allowed."

I watched my dad over the years as he enjoyed and loved Jamaica. I just wanted to be sitting on the veranda with him listening as he told me the same story as last year, but it didn't matter how often he told his stories because his timing and delivery were second to none, just like his cornmeal porridge. That porridge was so thick, the spoon could stand to attention. Listen, Goldilocks had nothing on my porridge. When my dad was going to say something important, he would take a deep breath and clasp his hands together and all you could do was sit there while he dropped those wise words. "Well, the position is this…" and you waited, because he was always right!

I really missed that my parents weren't just there anymore. They left in June and in July, I was in Jamaica, already missing them, trying to be a lost orphan. Over the years, my time spent in Jamaica grew longer; I would be there for Christmas and stay until March. The children had grown and my husband was relaxed about it. When their holiday was up and they left to go back to England, I would drive them to the airport with my dad. I'd wave them off and drive home with him; it was our time to just be together.

My dad was the coolest funniest man I know, he would drop a joke just like that; he had a very dry sense of humour. When he cracked a joke, he'd act as though he hadn't, it's only when you were on the floor with laughter that he'd smirked, and you'd think, *'So you knew that was funny.'* He never repeated his jokes, he would hit it just the once. If you missed it, that was it, you'd missed it. My comedic gift comes straight from my dad, he used his humour beautifully, he would make you feel loved and never excluded anyone. He didn't care who you were, a local MP, bishop, celebrity or a road sweeper, he treated you the same, and everyone loved him for that, they loved how he made them feel. I hear stories about my dad from people of different walks of life and they all describe him in the same way—an honest, hard-working, and I mean hard-working, man. I watched my dad come home from work, have dinner, and then go do another evening job, never complaining. Then he'd decorate the house and just do everything, he could fix anything, and make it look like it was his profession. He was a generous, loyal, and fair man, and very soft, especially to his grandchildren, he adored them. In Jamaica, he knew the children loved to play basketball, and that was all he needed to know, he had the basket loops fitted to the house, and would watch them as they played until it was dark. Not to worry, Granddad had night lights set up so they could play until it was late, then it would be time to let out the dogs. He thought of everything.

A local man said to me in Jamaica, "Your father always looked after me, he always give me lunch money." This was quickly followed by, "You have any can gi me?" This was my dad indeed.

My dad's legs started to fail him and walking up and down stairs became difficult, so he would keep stones on the veranda so he could wrap up $100 Jamaican dollars for those local friends in need…

He was a very protective man who looked after and raised his family. I have seen my dad lose his temper twice in my life and both times it was to protect my mother. If you upset my mother, hurt her or disrespected her, my dad wasn't having it. I was like, *'My dad is proper gangster too.'* He never stopped being protective. I'd go walking in Jamaica and if the rain started to fall and I wasn't near the house, I knew my dad would come and get me. Lo and behold, the rain would start and there was my dad, waiting with umbrella in hand.

A little girl in Jamaica would call me names as a joke as I passed her house, but my dad didn't like that she'd called me, "Dutty Angela". I laughed it off, I knew she was playing on the *Dirty Diana* song, but my dad didn't take too kindly to her chants and went over to her house and had a few words anyway. Can you imagine, me, 49-years-old, having to call my dad to have a few words with a five-year-old?

We saw love growing up. I am thankful to my mother because she taught me how to love my husband through her example. I had to make sure my dad's dinner was dished up in a particular way, in many serving bowls, which always baffled me—why couldn't all the food fit on one plate? My dad never forgot to thank my mother after each meal. He'd say, "That was lovely, thanks dear," and she'd reply, "Thank you for thanking me," after every single meal.

My father wasn't always a Christian, but I can confidently say I know my father is with God the Father right now, and I know he will be nudging God on my behalf.

My dad left me with the advice to be a real Christian and not a fake one. We all know it's easy to say you are a Christian, but living as one is not quite so easy. On his deathbed, he would say to me, "Be a spiritual Christian and not an educated one."

He wasn't playing at church. My father lived a great Christian life right to the end. He was an example, and that's how he became a Christian, through the examples of other Christians. When my mother was sick, the members of her church came to wash, cook, clean and pray with my family. My dad witnessed this and was touched by the love and kindness they showed. He knew that his worldly friends wouldn't do this and it was then, when they were praying, that he gave his heart to the Lord, not in a church. You see, you never know who is watching you; Christian life isn't just for Sunday.

One of my dad's favourite song lyrics was, *If I can help somebody as I pass along…then my living shall not be in vain.* Well it wasn't in vain at all!

I will say this, he was a great dad and I will miss him deeply. In those difficult times, I will go with my emotions. But I know what will bring me back, I'll remember my dad saying, "What are you crying for, Angela? Live your life, girl. You know I love you, don't moan for me, you did what you needed to do for me when I was alive." He always said that to me, even at the end. *Okay, Dad.*

I take comfort and feel privileged that he was my dad.

My loving father, Raglan George Martin. Love you forever, Dad X

My father walking me to the gazebo to be married.

The home that my parents built in Jamaica, called Faithvilla.

With my first born, Travis.

My family: David, Tyler, Tru and Travis.

Chapter 31:
The five Ts

Travis, Tyler, Tru, Tie, Tubes. I never thought I'd have kids, I don't know why I thought that. I mean, I like children, although I wasn't your babysitter type of person; I just couldn't see that as an option for making money. I loved to see little girls dressed up and cute babies smelling sweet and lovely. Boys, no thank you. I can't deal with their hard shoes, their energy and their need to know everything. Girls wanting to know was fine. If I was going to choose, I wanted girls.

After my second boy, I thought, *'No, is this for real, what's with the boys?'* Was I going to be like my Mum and have boys then one girl? After Tyler, I thought I wouldn't get the girl.

Travis was a really well-behaved baby. After the shock of the pregnancy and that entire saga, I finally settled down to being a mother. My seven days in hospital getting to know this baby, this baby that only took three hours to push out, was an experience no one can prepare you for. This baby is yours, he wants feeding and changing, he wants everything, and he wants you to do it. Soon I'm expressing all my milk to give me a bit of ease from the breastfeeding which wasn't enjoyable at first. I sleep on the expressing machine, I wake up and my breast is flat; I am so excited to get all the milk out. However, I wasn't expecting five times as much milk to come back; I'd work to get these hills off my chest, these rock-hard breasts! I screamed for the nurses, I looked at them and when they looked at me, they were smiling. The pain eased when I slowly filled up bottles for the premature baby unit. That's right, there are some healthy people out there who benefited from my breasts. Let's just leave it there.

After learning how not to get pregnant, I stayed not pregnant for eight years. Travis was a laid-back child, easy-going, fun-loving and calm; he stayed like that as a young man. He was always into something, playing basketball, sports, and he was always well-behaved, a very sensible child. Life was easy with Travis; in fact, he gave us the confidence to think we could do this again. So we planned our next child—our only planned child. Yes, we planned Tyler, we planned him, it was all in the plan. I get pregnant, I screamed just like they did in the movies, then we started to feel, *'Okay then! Why did we plan another child? We're not married and I am still living at home.'* These were things we hadn't considered because I wanted another baby.

It wasn't a bad pregnancy, although the heartburn was no joke, then Tyler was here, and boy did we know it. He was 8lb 2oz and came in three hours. Travis had been 7lb 10oz. Who was this big kid? I know people say children are individuals, they have their own minds and characters and you shouldn't compare them, but you do! I only had Travis as an example so forgive me if I wondered why this kid was so loud and rude. Why does this child answer me back? When Travis was hungry, he was polite. What five-month-old wakes up and throws his bottle at his parents when you're sleeping? Tyler.

When Tyler started school, I was more excited than he was because I wouldn't need to keep shouting, *'Tyler!'* all day, stopping fights, explaining once again why we don't do that. One afternoon, I left him screaming in his bouncer. I went into another room and cried because this child of mine wouldn't settle. As soon as his dad came home from work, I'd run to my room to get ready. I had a show to do, I had to de-stress and feel funny, I had to forget the day and get in the zone. The drive to the venue was always the break I needed, especially the local gigs. I could leave the children and get away. I stayed late at the shows, enjoying my freedom.

I was on stage once in Birmingham; my family was in the changing room with enough crisps and drinks to keep them going. I'm in full swing on stage, then the audience started laughing and I hadn't told a joke… No, it was Tyler standing behind me being all cute, thinking it was funny to do that. My mum would say, *'You're going to have a child like yourself, you'll know what it's like to have a child that causes concern.'* That child was Tyler.

When Tyler was in his second school, they had called me up to the school again. This time, they are going to put him on report. I accept that this might have to be the last resort. On the way home, I questioned him. "Why can't you behave yourself? Do you know you're at school to learn? What is wrong with you?" He just looked at me, not even puzzled, "It's the teachers!"

I sit there listening to the teacher on parents evening, and to be honest, there were times when I knew the teachers were thinking, *'What kind of mother is this? How come she's not taking this seriously?'* I tried, but the truth was they were describing me. They could have just said, "Angie is constantly trying to be the class clown." Tyler was very disruptive, but he was such a charming boy. He was so charming, he managed to get his teacher to change four out of ten to nine out of ten. I spoke to her and she honestly said, "But it's *Tyler*, he's so sweet!"

Tyler was now going to be schooled at home. He was going to get the best! Travis was quiet and got on with life; Tyler was a joke a minute. The time we spent at home, we really bonded, we did everything together. He attended all my meetings, giving me his opinion about business. He can cook most dishes, he can clean house, he wasn't going to just do lessons at home and then sleep, we had gardening to do, the dog to walk; yes, I worked him.

Tru reminds me of Travis but looks like Tyler. She was born in about 12 minutes, a caesarean due to illness. She was a beautiful baby, no squashed face here, piercing dark eyes, a little pudding. Tru wasn't into dolls which annoyed me. I bought her so many black dolls on my travels. She was polite about them and left them there on the bed. She went through a quick phase of dolls, but it was so quick and I was grateful for that little time. When it was over, it was over, I couldn't convince her.

One day the school was doing a collection for the jumble sale. I saw the bag she was taking to give away—yes, I have raised my children to give generously to those in need, but, "Tru, this is ridiculous! You can't give all your dolls away!" I had a doll collection, if she didn't want them, why couldn't she give them to me? That night, I went into the bag and swapped some of the dolls with old toys and hid them. I got to the jumble sale early and bought them back. I know what you're thinking and I don't care, they're mine. I searched high and low for those dolls.

Raising children is no joke; they make you feel all kinds of emotions, being protective is standard. I was the kind of mother who walked into the school if you even thought about bullying my children. I was not the mother to write letters, I'd walk straight to the child and ask where their parents were, I'd walk up to the parents and say, "We have a problem, Houston. Your child is bullying my child, we can do the parents take control thing, or I'm going to have my child do what their dad taught them to do, and that is a big worry." We always came to an agreement.

Do you ever stop worrying about your children? No. The different stages they go through will allow it to ease, but today's generation of young people are under some serious pressure; just walking down the wrong street could be dangerous for them… As much as you try to guide them and show them the rights and wrongs, it is still going to be their choice in the end.

I'm happy with what makes my children confident and happy and that they are doing that in the best way they know. When my Travis said he wanted to be a comedian, I was rather surprised; he's been a quiet child, and didn't show any signs of being a performer. If you'd said Tyler or Tru, yes, I could see that because they are funny all the time. But Travis went on stage and I was shocked. I thought, *'Where did that come from, you little dark horse?'* When I was pregnant with Travis, I did stand-up right through my pregnancy, so he was with me gigging a long time.

When it's time for them to leave home, nothing can prepare you for walking into their empty room; the silence is deafening. I used to think, *'When the kids leave, it will be our time to chill, no stress, no noise, just peace.'* If I could choose, I'd have the noise and stress. The laughter in my home was on all day, every day; we all had jokes, we were all funny, and we all wanted to laugh. As a family, we could entertain ourselves. In fact, whenever the doorbell rang, we always felt disturbed; there were quick questions: "Are you expecting anyone?" We were heartbroken to have visitors sometimes.

We are a family that celebrated each other; to this day, every birthday is celebrated. We'll go out to dinner. You're not allowed to miss each other's birthday, it's that person's special day, and we all have to make a speech about why we think they are special: you must be there!

The boys will come home often. I think it's to get topped up because there is no place like home, the food and the encouragement is so nurturing. This is the place where we keep safe, the home you can return to let go and refuel. The father and son talks are the funniest, especially when Dave has to say, "The thing about women that you have to understand…" while I'm sitting there.

As for my daughter, when she talks about moving out, we just get more nails and start banging, we feed her through a hole in the wall and she seems very happy. That is one day I'm not looking forward to; yes, it's great that we have raised them well, to go out into the world and become their greatest self, but it's sad. Don't get me wrong, I will get over it, I guess. If I had known I would feel this, I would have had more children.

My children are my success story, they make me proud, and I hope they are as proud of me.

Chapter 32:
Pinch me

There are some times in life when you have to ask someone to pinch you. I have had a few of those moments and I have always been so grateful for the opportunities that work has afforded me.

All my life, I had watched Whoopi Goldberg. She taught me so much without her knowing a thing about it. Watching her as a comedienne and as an actress was all I needed; she was my indirect mentor. I have watched most of her work from when I was a young girl. I was inspired by this edgy woman with locks who didn't seem to care. Her work was outstanding; she spoke about things that most people would shy away from. Her Broadway show turned me into Whoopi's biggest fan. I got the chance to interview her when she was over in London to promote her book. Only Whoopi could call her book *Book*.

I had to interview her, it became a mission. I was at BBC GLR at the time so I could use the BBC title bit and sound a bit like TV. We were given 15 minutes, no more, no less, and that was going to be my time with the lady who had inspired me in so many ways. I was working on *Get Up Stand Up* at the time and got on so well with the crew that I asked them, "If I were to get an interview with Whoopi Goldberg, would you film it for me?" They were all up for it. This was a top crew; I was so surprised they agreed. Now all I needed to do was get Whoopi's team to agree, and they did. I had a crew and a Hollywood star. Everyone was in place at Planet Hollywood, make-up, hair, camera… I was so nervous. My friend John Byrne had helped me with this. I had written a poem for Whoopi and we'd framed it, I wanted her to know what she meant to me.

Whoopi walks in. I nearly collapse, I am just lost for a few seconds. Then I have the nerve to say, "Whoopi, as we are filming this, can we just start with me reading from your book, and then you walk over to me, and say, 'Angie!' I look up and I'm shocked that it's you." Whoopi says, "Sure, Angie, let's do it." Her agent looks at me, as if to say, *'How on earth did you pull that off?'* I'm telling you, I was as shocked as her. The interview that was supposed to be for 15 minutes went on for an hour and a half. We laughed and we joked. I told her that *The Color Purple* was my all-time favourite film. I added that story about how I had been stood up on the date when I was supposed to go and see it. I told her I'd cried so hard over that film. Whoopi looks into the camera, stares down the lens and says, "Clive, how dare you stand Angie up. Look at her now!" That moment right there, priceless!

It's always your fear that when you meet someone you admire, they are going to fall short of what you had imagined in your mind, but Whoopi was more than I had imagined.

Then there was the interview with Terry McMillan. I was warned, "Terry does not suffer fools. If you haven't read her book, she won't be interested in talking to you." But I hadn't finished the book, *A Day Late and a Dollar Short*. Terry was due on my radio show. I had to try and get as much into my head overnight as I could; I started calling friends to give me their take. I am powering through this book, I will not be caught short with Terry, she will not be upset with my review or interview.

I'm a big fan of Terry and I have to say that although she has a warm and inviting presence, she can also be very intimidating, she just doesn't look like she has time to waste. The station was waiting for Terry, she arrives, the interview starts, and that's it, we hit it off. She compliments me on my skin and my hair. I was growing locs at the time and had my wig on, so when I explained this, we were laughing and joking like old friends. In fact, I met her the following day. I've found that if I can get my guests laughing, we tend to have a great interview. If only she'd known how shattered I was that day because I'd been up all night reading her book. That was one of my favourite interviews.

My Saturday morning show was very popular; it was often number one at the weekends, so it made sense that if you had something to sell, you'd get on Angie's show. One day I received a call from a friend asking me to do her a big favour. Her friend was over doing a concert, but no promotion had been done. Could I get her on the station? Well my show was booked up that Saturday, but I told her to bring her in and I'd squeeze her on. I remember this singer walking in, a lovely woman, but her hair was a rusty red colour and I had never seen it before. It suited her; it was like it was her natural colour.

She came on and I promoted her show as best I could. She was pleased, and it was a success. Fast forward, I am broadcasting live from the jazz festival in St Lucia. I'm relaxing at my hotel villa with my husband, I'm in my nightie, it's a nice one, so I can go outside in it and lounge. Then out of the corner of my eye, I see this woman walking slowly over to me. I thought nothing of it until she got closer and said, "Hi, Angie, you don't remember me, but years ago I was on your show. You helped me out at a time when I really needed it. I never forgot that. Can I repay you by introducing you to Isaac Hayes over there?"

It's only when I was walking over to Isaac Hayes with my husband that I realised I was still wearing my nightie. I did not care, this was a moment! I didn't have time to change my clothes. The legend that was this great man, he was so polite and kind to us both.

There are times when people just want to say thank you for your kindness. Sometimes you think you've done a little thing, but it might have been just what was needed in that person's life. I had one of Prince's backing singers on my show; I gave her a lot of love for her brilliant album. She wanted to thank me by giving me front row tickets to see Prince. We were in the front row; Naomi Campbell was on my right. I was close enough to Prince for his sweat to fall on me. What a great thank you present! I was so excited when I left with my husband; we'd had a great night, and it was such a kind gesture. Then the following day, I got a call from my new friend asking where I'd got to after the show; why hadn't I come backstage to meet Prince with my VIP pass? When I told my husband about what could have been, he walked silently away. I had failed dramatically. Even now as I remember this, I have to go and lie down for five minutes…

Whenever dark is dawning and the music of the midnight starts to play…just give me the night. I love George Benson, so when we heard he was going to be in London the following year, we bought tickets so far in advance that we could only hope we'd still be alive when the time came. Then one afternoon, my husband called and asked me to check the dates on the George Benson tickets. His friend had gone to see George the night before so he wondered if he was doing two nights. With my heart beating fast, I walked over to the drawer and opened the envelope. I had to take a deep breath as I took the ticket out. There weren't two shows, we'd missed the concert. We'd been so keen to go. We'd done the right thing, we'd booked in advance! But we'd forgotten.

I picked the phone up and whispered, "It was yesterday, goodbye, Dave." I couldn't talk, this was George Benson, and he was going to give me the night… It was a difficult evening; there were a lot of dirty looks.

Then I was asked to broadcast in St Lucia again and I got to watch George live. So as I'm a little hustler, I have to get an interview with the legend. I'm in the VIP section, but there is another section that I can't get into. As I stand there, who should walk by? John Legend, all these legends! He shouts out, "Angie!" and tells the security to let me in. I walked in and thanked John. He remembered me from the interview I did with him on Choice FM. I did a quick interview with John, and then I went and found George Benson. We started the interview and he calls his friend over to join us. Who is this friend? The amazing Al Jarreau. What can you say…

My ultimate pinch me moment was meeting Maya Angelou. I can only describe it as a moment I will never forget; it was an inspiring interview. Being in her presence felt almost spiritual; she had a presence that I had never experienced with any of the stars I'd met over the years. When you meet Maya Angelou, you want to curtsy to her, it's like meeting a queen. I went to shake her hand and I bowed my head. She stopped me and said, "Angie, do not bow to anyone except God."

After reading her books for years, when I finally got to talk to her, I had all these questions inside that I wanted answered, some of them personal, because I knew she would have the answers to many of my questions about life. She was a beautiful woman and she told me that she worked on being a Christian every day. It was one of those interviews that I never wanted to end. She was more than inspiring; she truly was a phenomenal woman.

I'm sure when I walked into the room filled with agents and bodyguards, Stevie Wonder looked at me. *'Of course he didn't, Angie, he's blind.'* When I interviewed this great man, I felt he was looking at me; I kept forgetting he was blind. His energy was awesome, I was so blown away by him, and it felt like sitting with a friend. I told him it was my birthday, and he sang *Happy Birthday* to me. I was in such shock, I must have frozen. His agent looked at me, like, *'How dare you?'* I'm thinking, *'I know, how dare me.'* I have always believed you have one shot, they will say yes or no. Stevie sang to me and no one can ever take that away.

There is something about him. When you listen to his music, hear him talk, it's a bit like he has a special power; he was sent here to do something and he is doing his assignment. It's more than a musical gift that Stevie has; it feels like more than music to me. I left that interview and listened to some of his music. No need to pinch me then, I wouldn't have felt it.

My inspiration, comedienne and talk show host, Whoopi Goldberg.

With singer George Benson at St Lucia Jazz Festival.

With George Benson and Al Jarreau at St Lucia Jazz Festival.

My producer Patience Chinwada and myself broadcasting live from
St Lucia Jazz Festival.

With singer John Legend at Choice FM.

The late great activist and author, amongst so many titles, Maya Angelou.

Singer songwriter Stevie Wonder, just after he sang Happy Birthday to me.

I told you about me and Gayle King. Here we are at the O Magazine Offices
in New York. She has no idea who I am, for now.

Choice FM, *The Ladies Room Talk Show,* which lead to the
Saturday morning show.

On the radio.

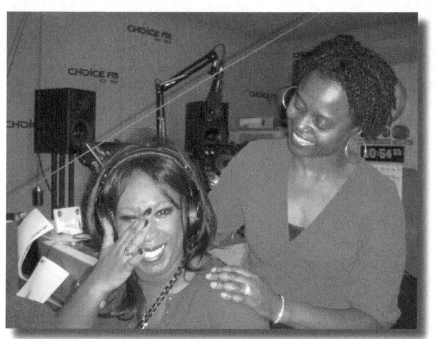

After years of listening to the amazing voice of Jean Adebambo,
I was so emotional when she called my home to say she was coming
on my last show. I can't tell you what that meant to me.
A few months later, she was gone, RIP.

The Angie Le Mar Show on Premier Gospel with Marcia Dixon and special guest Lurine Cato.

Chapter 33:
Faith

I f you had told me a couple of years ago that I was going to end up back in church, I would have said, "I know I am supposed to get back into the church, but I don't know whether I am going back just yet." I mean, I love God and all that, but I couldn't.

How did I get back to church? Well God has always been a part of my life, with all that I was raised with it really wasn't going to leave me, but those early memories of going to church were etched in my brain. Even when I was sick and I had that close conversation with God, it seemed that after coming through that, I should have gone back, but I still didn't go back to church.

But even then something in my life was changing. I wasn't as interested in the things that had used to really inspire me. I wasn't as desperate to make it, the productions, the celebrities, the parties, the endless networking; the meetings that didn't do anything more than waste my time. The many lunches and dinners that only served to put on weight. I wasn't depressed. At least, I didn't feel depressed until much later. I used to sit and stare out of the window, sit there for hours, and only tried to look busy when my family came home from school and work. Something was missing and I couldn't quite work it out.

I would write my gratitude list and this list was truly impressive; there were so many wonderful things I was grateful for. But each day felt like a chore. I felt like, *'What am I going to do? I need to make it through this long, boring day. Who do I need to contact? I need something.'* I couldn't snap out of it. I felt low and, at times, very lonely.

Who knew that my anniversary present from my husband, a chocolate Labrador puppy, would be the gift I needed? Oh, I was so in love with my dog. I loved taking Luther Soul on walks in the park. I loved the way he needed me, the way he loved me, I loved my dog.

The long walks in the park connected me with nature. I made new friends among the other dog owners. They only talk to you if you have a dog, that's what you need to get into this club. It's a club you go to twice a day, it was my new rave. It could be snowing or raining, nothing stops us; Luther Soul needs walking.

All that nature around me on the walks must have inspired the gardener in me because I suddenly started to grow green fingers. I was so busy with my dog and garden, that at times I'd actually forget to cook dinner. I'd be in the garden, and then I'd have to take Luther for his evening walk. I'll cook when I get back; sometimes I would start dinner at around 9 pm. The days were getting better. Maybe I'd just needed to be needed, and Luther needed me, the plants needed me. I felt so much better.

I contacted a friend and said, "You know what, I'm a bit concerned about my addiction to gardening, it's just not like me." She said, "You may be rooting up old stuff in your life. You're doing it physically, weeding it all out. Now you are sowing new seeds." Oh, okay. It made sense to me, I was truly weeding a lot of things out of my life, and some of it was done unconsciously. I didn't need the things that I'd needed before, I didn't need to be in the know, or popular. I'd even lost the need to buy shoes…something was definitely going on.

I would look at my lawn and the beautiful flowers and just be in awe. I kept thinking about the seeds that I had sown, and then weeks later these flowers were looking back at me. It lifted my spirits; I was slowly coming to feel that the world was a wonderful place. Something had been missing before, things didn't impress me anymore. I'd needed something deeper, a seed needed to be planted so that something new could grow. Feeling inspired, I wanted to write. I wanted to get back on the stage.

I've always wanted to do a one-woman show with various characters. I wanted to stretch myself, so I wrote my very first character-based one-woman show *In My Shoes*. I had a producer and a director on board, I had a venue, and I was back in the Angie lane. All was going well; we had a few struggles with next to no budget, but I was determined that this show would sell. Let's do a four-week run in the heart of the West End; it would be a great comeback as I had been off the scene for a bit. I was excited, still under pressure, but hey, let's go for it.

The production was going to be an uphill struggle, but I felt confident. I was worried about the budget and the show's cost was creeping up, but my audience wouldn't let me down. I was praying they were keen to see me do something different. I got a call from my producer. He said the show had been cancelled; they were not going to do it because somebody else wanted to use the space, a bigger production. I thought, *'Well you can't. We have sent out the press releases, we have sent out everything, flyers, the posters, all done.'* He told me that it was pretty much a done deal, they had done it.

I woke up the next morning and went downstairs. I sat in my dining room and started to write myself a letter called *I am somebody*. I wrote a list: *I am somebody's daughter, somebody's mother, somebody's wife, somebody's sister, somebody's friend, I am somebody.* Why do people treat people like this, why am I going through this? I wasn't only writing about the show, I was writing about my life and I was facing all my disappointments that morning.

When you keep going after all the rejections, after the hurt and pain, you have to put it somewhere. Then it starts to affect you, it wears you down, it's like you're lugging this thing around your neck, it's something you should have put down, but put down where? We mastered our feelings, we dusted ourselves down and we got on with it, we kept moving. But I was finally tired and the mask was slipping off. I was going to face it all this Saturday morning.

There was a song playing on a gospel channel called The Potter's House, which contained the line *The potter wants to put you back together again.* I just cried and cried. Old tears. Not for the show, no show could make me cry like that. I was crying for my sickness, the disappointments, let-downs, lies, deceit, betrayals, the loss of friendship, the mistakes, and the never-ending rejections. The crying was too much; I couldn't stop myself. My husband came in and said, "It's going to be alright."

After he left, the tears I'd tried to bottle up came flooding back. I called my mum in Jamaica and said, "Mum, I can't do this. I don't know what's wrong with me, I'm not happy anymore and I can't fix it. The show has been cancelled and I can't think of what to do. I thought this was going to be it for me. I don't know who I am anymore."

Mum said, "Put the phone down, I am going to pray." When my mum says she is going to pray, it's on, get behind Satan, Sister Martin is onto you. So I put the phone down. My producer calls me about five minutes later with the news that the show is back on.

"What?"

So I called my mum back. "Mum, the show is back on."

"Yes, I know. I told God I wanted an immediate response."

"Well...amen."

Then she said it, "Angie, go to church tomorrow. Put yourself in that church and give thanks."

I said, "No problem. That's a small thing to do."

The next day, I tried to get my children to come to church with me and they wouldn't get up and kept saying no. They were raised in church too, but they hadn't been trained like me. There was a church nearby with a pastor who used to go to my old church when I was growing up, so I went there. It felt great being back, the singing, and the memories. I sat there and I saw someone who used to be my best friend in Sunday school. *'My God, it's Pamela, after all these years!'* I'd loved Pamela and here she was back at church. Was she visiting like me, or was she really back? I said, "Oh my God, Pamela, look at you! What are you doing here?"

"I am back in the church now." I felt really pleased for Pamela, she looked happy. Then an American preacher came on, and guess what his theme was? "I am somebody."

The preacher was so powerful, it was exactly what I needed, and it was so in keeping with what I had been going through. I was feeling it was a good move to come to church today, but then he started saying, "We need writers in the church, we need people who can teach the young girls what to do. Christians in the music and media business need to guide them in the industry. We don't want half-naked girls on the front covers."

I am looking at him, and thinking, *'He doesn't know me and he can't see me.'* But it felt like it was aimed at me. He said, "You need to be strong in what you are doing. You have to do something special, you have come to change people's lives and you have to give your life to God. You've got to turn it around."

At the end, he gives an altar call and I'm saying to myself I know the altar call number and I am not doing it. So after a while, he goes and sits down, and I think, *'Phew!'* Then he gets up again and says, "You know who you are, you got to get down here today." He was serious. He was talking to me.

I just felt myself get up; I seemed to be walking to the altar on autopilot. I didn't have anything to do with it, my body had made the decision; it was time.

I got up and gave my heart to the Lord and then my old friend, Pastor Roy McLeod, said, "This is a very special day for me because I grew up with

Angie. We went to the same church when we were children. I've known her since she was a little girl."

They were looking at me like, "Ain't that Angie Le Mar?" I was feeling very awkward...

I got home really excited, and I said to my husband, "Dave, I am a Christian."

"What?"

"I am a Christian and I've got to do the right thing now."

The funniest thing is it didn't feel like it was a big shift because I wasn't very different from who I am now. I wasn't saved from the brink of madness or some sinful life. I was now committed to Christ and I said to myself, "Look at Pamela and me. We are sitting in church, sharing sweets. When we were younger, we used to share sweets in church."

I asked her, "Pam, how did you get here?"

She said, "It was time. This is where it's peaceful and my life has changed. This is where I have always belonged."

Then my life started changing. People were brought to me, doors were being opened and I thought, *'God you have had a hand in my life for a long time.'* I went to Jamaica and my mum is really excited that I am now a Christian. I'm baptised and she watches the video and says, "Oh, I have been praying for this for years."

God has always been guiding me to where I am. There have been some near misses in my life. I had to learn to be grateful that I didn't get some of the things I wanted. That forced me to do something else. The play that I didn't get became the play I wrote and so on. This has been my life; what I have missed out on led me to create something original. He was trying to say to me, "You were born to create; you are not supposed to be given crumbs. Bake your own bread."

The Angie Le Mar School of Expression. I was able to gather a great team of management and teachers to teach the arts. A truly inspirational time.

If Jeffrey Daniels from the hit group Shalamar could teach Michael Jackson the moonwalk, then why couldn't I ask my dear friend to come to the school to teach our students. A great time it was too.

Speaking at the UNESCO conference at the University of Connecticut.

Ladies Talk TV. Inspired by appearance on ITV's *Loose Women.*
Myself with presenters and broadcasters and journalist Jacqui Joseph,
Jasmine Dotiwala and Jackie G Michaels.

Hosting my TV Show *Ladies Talk*.

Chapter 34:
Lessons learned so far…

You have only learned your lessons when you truly get what you were supposed to learn. There have been many times when I thought I'd learned my lesson, only to repeat the same mistake over and over again. My biggest lesson is to never ever give up on myself, to keep getting up and keep going. It's only when you get up that you realise how much you learned when you were down.

I also understand that with great expectations, there can be great disappointments. But I must never give up on people. We've all been hurt, we've all had broken hearts and dreams. I've been let down by close friends, been devastated by family. Sometimes it's shocking what people are capable of, but you have to heal yourself or you will go under and become bitter and never get over it. I have gone through difficult times when I've felt that I have no more trust left. I can't do the disappointment, the let-down again, I can't trust again; it hurts too much. You start to protect yourself by trusting no one, then someone sneaks through and it happens all over again. I used to think I was stupid. *'Why did that happen again? I really trusted that one; they convinced me that they were different.'*

When someone does me wrong, I don't always confront them. I used to if I wanted to repair the friendship, but as times goes by, you realise there wasn't anything to repair. Some people don't like you, so it's best to remove yourself and forgive them.

Forgiveness must be the ultimate lesson to learn. It is a must-do on your personal to-do list. Even if you can't do it face to face with someone who has hurt you, you can make that peace privately. That's what is so powerful about forgiveness; you can do it from a distance. So I have learned not to take things to heart, just remain who I am, soul intact, and keep it moving.

Being kind is standard; it takes nothing to be kind. Sadly, you meet some people who are truly unkind. More often than not, they are hiding some kind of insecurity, or they've lied about their skills or their lives and don't want to be unmasked. When you get too close, their character barks as they are about to be exposed.

I'm always uncomfortable around dismissive and unkind people; it's a nasty trait that I cannot accept. I have been with people who treat others as though they were lesser beings. I have learned that if someone treats the waiter or the cleaner disrespectfully, we are not going to get on together. I have gone against my instincts before; I met those who thought maybe we could work together. Then I watched how they treated people in different situations, which is always very telling. If you see that behaviour, it's just a matter of time before they turn it onto you.

There have been many times I have had to go home and stare out the window, one of those '*What just happened?*' moments. So you trusted again, after you were warned, there are people who blame you for being too soft, the ones who tell you to toughen up, but the truth is you are tough, and you just need to be sure. Honestly, life is too short to have to be worried about something that your gut already told you to watch out for. There is no need to second guess our gut instincts; we need to listen to them because they are never wrong. They can't lie; they're not faking it to wind you up. It's hard when something goes wrong, especially when you want the other thing that person has to offer. But you will walk away eventually so you may as well walk away early. My mum used to say, "My mind did tell me." Yes. We'd already been warned. We all feel it, so trust it.

When you are wrong, have the sense and good character to say sorry. We don't always get it right, sometimes we upset people, we say the wrong thing, our tone is off, or we miss them out in a certain situation. Sometimes it's not your fault. I have fallen out with people over stupid things, misunderstandings; I have been confronted by hurt people, people who were expecting me to do something, for them, or with them. Maybe I didn't return an email or make a job offer. I didn't come to see them in a show, I didn't cast them in my plays, and they felt ignored. The list goes on and in some cases, it has been so petty. But I have to also try and understand what it meant to them, because it might have been a big deal for them. It could have been an innocent mistake on my behalf, or maybe I was weary and didn't follow through, or maybe I just messed up! I can only apologise. It was never my intention to hurt them.

Intention is one of those powerful words; once I understood this word, everything made sense. It helped me look at life from a great place. When I received strong criticism, I can look at the intention behind it. I have used it when reading my reviews and it has helped me understand if the critics wanted me to improve my writing, acting, productions, or whatever. I can work through their words to their intentions. Words are powerful. The truth is that we upset people, but if it honestly wasn't your intention, then rest well. If you knew deep down that you wanted your words to make someone feel uncomfortable and then pretend that you didn't, well, your intentions weren't good, so don't expect it to go well.

Reason, season or lifetime, that's friendships in a nutshell. It's hard to accept when good friendships break up. I have had some wonderful friends; I always believed that if we were good friends, then why shouldn't the relationship just go on forever? Well, not all should. I truly understand that some friendships are to do with where you are in your life at that moment and those friends are there for that period. When you are through that moment, the friendship is over. Even if you've shared some special moments, some secrets, when the time has passed then it's time to move on from this friendship.

Then you have friends that no matter where you go in life, you care about how they are. You don't have to see them often, years go by, but when you meet, it's like yesterday. Those friendships have no expectations attached, so you can't let each other down. It's really important to know where you put people.

Some friends are like microwaves; you meet quickly, you work really well together and enjoy each other and then it's over. That's okay; you may just have wanted a quickie friendship. Then there are the friends who want to be your twin; they really just want to be you and live your life. They get very close to you, they are involved in everything, they offer to help you, they're very over the top, and you start to get annoyed with them. You start to irritate each other. They start hating you because you make all your hard work look too easy, and you're not helping them to become you fast enough, so they resent you. The friendship ends, and you avoid each other at events! Then they tell everybody how you stopped them because you were jealous. Here's how you deal with those: forgive them and move on.

As I have got older, I've often wondered about the obstacles we faced in show business, the struggles that seem to reinvent themselves with every generation. I wonder if we did enough. Could we have done more from the 70s until now to bring change? I have accepted that we can't change people by saying that we are just like you and we are all a part of the human race. I don't think that's enough anymore. If anything, I think it has gotten worse today and the people we are trying to convince about diversity and multiculturalism don't really care! Okay, maybe a few do. To live in a world where you have to keep proving yourself can be exhausting, but we can never give up the fight.

My parents' generation trusted each other to put money into a pardner every week to help each and everyone, one by one, to buy their own homes. There was no jealousy or resentment, they were just happy that you got yours, and trusted that they would get theirs too.

It's that level of trust and patience that will build us up. I don't think there's any point in asking for help from someone who is already not giving you what is due to you. Why expect them to do anything? Calling them racists won't get them to listen or change. They know it is racism, they know what they are doing. The people you meet about your work are the same people clutching their bags when they see your son. There is no special black person in their eyes, and I am so tired of black people thinking they can have a quick word on our behalf: it does not work. They don't care! Okay, maybe the odd one.

History tells us that leaders got those roles because they created solutions and fixed problems. If you can change a heart, then you can change a mind, but to just change a mind is an absolute waste of time, because it's only a matter of time before they change it back. When we were not allowed in their clubs, we created our own. We built restaurants, and we built businesses within our communities. Then one day we were fooled into believing that they liked us, and we were so glad to be accepted. After all we have achieved and shared, what do we have to show for it? It should be ownership we are after, not acceptance. We can't keep learning the same lesson. Now more than ever, we need to be aware that we are on the same side; if we don't work together, we are pretty much working against ourselves.

I am not trying to be you, and I love that you are you, but sometimes it turns into a competition… I have to accept someone is funnier than me and I am funnier than someone else, but there is room for us all. Social networking has turned us a bit mad; this need to be liked, the need to look good, look at me at this event, ain't I better than you for being invited! I have seen that obsession in myself at times. It's time-consuming and it's a waste of life. Sometimes I threaten to delete all my networks, but then I think, *'How will I cope?'*

I read happy people are those who are not on Facebook and other social media networks. I tried it, I came off Facebook for a few months and honestly I was so much happier; there was an instant feeling of relief, like I had climbed off a treadmill. Comparison is a deadly thing; you see someone doing something you want to do, and you think, *'Oh, they've done it now.'* Then you see a group of friends that were out last night, and you think, *'Well no one told me.'* It is just ridiculous. So I limited myself. I do what I need to do, then I'm gone, no scrolling down. I set myself a time limit and then I go back to my real life, talking to people who actually move and speak back.

After I had a little scare last year, health became my priority. It used to come and go, especially in early January with the pressure to be better this year and then later that month, it would all go out the window. But as you get older, it becomes more serious; health is very important to me now. I now have 'three free-for-me hours.' This happens every day. I used to give so much of myself and burn myself out, but now I don't, I look after me first. I take my three hours first before I talk to anyone: no emails, texts, nothing to cloud my mind. I pray to centre myself with God, I walk with my dog, then I walk down to the swimming baths and swim 50 lengths. Swimming is such a great exercise, every muscle is being worked, and I feel so alive after a great swim. I have a quick sauna on some days. That's what I give to myself every day. Once I have done that, I can take the calls and do what is needed. I have burned the candles at both ends throughout my life and I am truly grateful that I am still doing what I love. I don't feel under pressure to be anything other than peaceful. As my mother has always said, "What is for you cannot be un for you." It's already written.

Chapter 35:
Church stand-up

Who knew? My mother knew. She had always believed that I would be doing stand-up comedy in the church. She would say to me, "You'll be doing comedy in the church; God will use you in the church." I thought that was a strange idea. I could only picture the church I grew up in, and as there was not much laughter in my church, where could I possibly fit in? I had the world to conquer and I didn't think the church wanted me anyway.

When I became a Christian, I happily got on with my life; I was happy to go to church. I saw it as separate to the work I did elsewhere. I had been a Christian for a few years when I was contacted by a very well-known and respected Christian PR and marketing person, Marcia Dixon. I had read Marcia's columns over the years in *The Voice* and *Keep the Faith*. She had also done a cover story interview with me about my faith.

Marcia and I had become good friends and one day she said she wanted to ask me something. I was keen to find out so we met for lunch. After a lovely lunch, Marcia put her suggestion to me. "Have you considered doing stand-up in the church?"